RESCUIN[illegible]E

A Gu[illegible]e to Helping Injured and Orphaned Animals

PEGGY SUE HENTZ

RED CREEK WILDLIFE CENTER, INC.

Published by:

Red Creek Wildlife Center, Inc.
300 Moon Hill Drive
Schuylkill Haven, PA 17972
www.RedCreekWildlifeCenter.com

Second Edition

Cover design by Peggy Sue Hentz

Photographs on pages iii, xiv, 47, 50, 51, 54, 70, 123 © Kathy Miller, www.CelticSunrise.com

Additional photographs by Peggy Sue Hentz, Barbara Miller, Lynn Dierwechter, Morrie Katz, Linda Martzall, Katie May Shultz, Lori Chylack, Ray Stone, Andrew (Corky) Hanzok, Jr.

ISBN-13: 978-1545036631

ISBN-10: 1545036632

DEDICATION

This book is dedicated to Morrie Katz.

Morrie and I wrote the first version of this book, "HELP! I FOUND AN ANIMAL," together. I did the writing, and he edited and rewrote everything so that all was "proper."

Much of my writing reflects what I learned from his example, and he sparked an interest in me to share my knowledge through the written word.

Morrie helped Red Creek grow from a small, part-time animal rescue to the thriving wildlife center that it is today. His mark is everywhere and in everything we do and is definitely found throughout this book.

He was also the bravest person I've ever known. While fighting a two-year battle with esophageal cancer, he continued to present live raptor programs at schools and events and manned the 24-hour wildlife emergency hotline late into the night.

Morrie was my life partner and the love I never thought I would experience. I miss him, and so does Red Creek. The world is a much better place because he spent some time in it.

DISCLAIMER

Personal contact with wildlife is accompanied by many dangers, including those that are mentioned throughout this book. The guidelines in this book are meant to help reduce these risks but cannot eliminate them. Instructions in this book neither imply nor promise absence of risk, and it is the reader's responsibility to use his or her best judgment in any actions undertaken.

Wildlife rehabilitation is regulated by both state and federal agencies. Regulations differ from one area to another, and not all jurisdictions allow for the rehabilitation of all species. It is the reader's responsibility to learn and follow the laws pertaining to his or her locality.

The reader takes full responsibility for his or her actions and choices, whether that choice is to follow the guidelines and instructions set forth in this book or not. The author, publisher and any and all agents involved in the production of this book shall not be held legally responsible for any consequences resulting from the reader's actions.

CONTENTS

ACKNOWLEDGEMENTS

This book could not have been written without the help of many individuals.

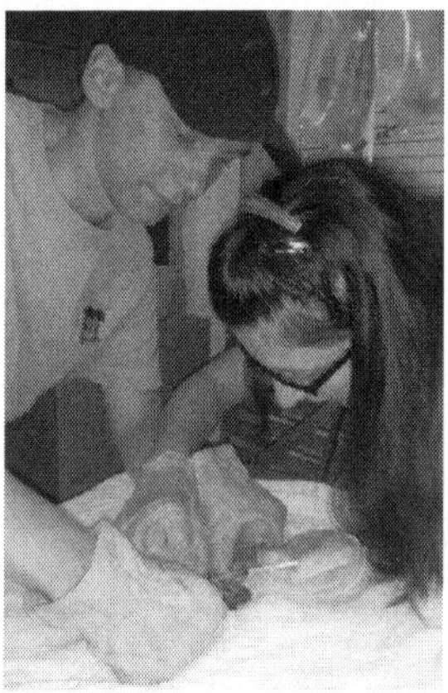

Greg Nason and Kat Hummel giving fluids to a red bat.

Foremost, I wish to acknowledge Greg Nason and Kat Hummel, Red Creek's newest licensed wildlife rehabilitators, who have embraced Red Creek's missions as their own, thus freeing up my time so I can write and teach, helping even more animals. In addition, Allison Rusinko, our newest rehabilitation assistant, helps with all facets of running Red Creek as well as with the animal care.

Wildlife rehabilitation is multifaceted and demanding. Many permit holders burn out, and their centers close after just a few years. Volunteers can be the difference between a rehabilitator's staying open or closing forever. All of Red Creek's volunteers and interns are dedicated to the care of our wildlife patients and work long hours to ensure their well-being. Amanda Roshannon, Bonnie Bohnenblust, and Mike Witman have served Red Creek for a decade or more, adding a consistency of care and knowledge so valuable to this work.

Sandra Taglieri has been a long-time supporter of Red Creek. She and her husband, Julius, volunteer to help with administrative tasks. Sandra proofs my writing and makes what I want to say understandable so that you can enjoy our publications without aggravation.

And last, but in no way the least, wildlife rehabilitators rely on generous public donations to support the service. Andy Muller and the Reading and Northern Railroad in Port Clinton, Pennsylvania cover one-half of Red Creek's operating expenses annually, and they have done so since 2008. If not for their generous contributions, Red Creek might have closed years ago. Because of their passion for wildlife, we've been able to remain open even during tough economic times, ensuring that our rehabilitation and education missions remain available to everyone.

INTRODUCTION

It can happen quite unexpectedly on any given day. You are going about your business of work, family, and life, and suddenly a wild animal interrupts everything. It could be a baby bird on your porch or an injured squirrel in the street. It could be presented to you by a child or a pet. However it happens, this hapless creature becomes the center of your life for a short time and, if you care about animals (as I assume you do because you are reading this book), you want to do something – anything – to help.

The choices you make will have an impact on that animal's life and possibly on your own. Having knowledge about the risks to the animal as well as to you, your family, and your pets, along with the right advice from the beginning can mean the difference between a heartwarming, educational experience and disaster.

I am a licensed wildlife rehabilitator. Every day I answer calls concerning foundling animals. The time it takes from the initial discovery until my phone rings can vary from moments to weeks, and that time often determines what we can (and cannot) do for the animal and the family involved.

During these calls, I often listen to the trials a person has gone through to find help: the numerous telephone calls with little or no guidance, the research that led to inaccurate information, and the attempts they made to care for the animal themselves. Many never knew that wildlife rehabilitators existed until someone pointed them my way.

In today's age of information, every subject can be researched on the internet. Many people start their search for help there and end up following incorrect or incomplete advice on how to treat an injured animal or raise a baby animal themselves. They are often devastated when an animal dies or suffers because of failed attempts to help it.

What they do not learn about are the many problems which may beset the animal even after an apparently "successful" release of that animal into the wild. Good nutrition and suitable husbandry, along with developing appropriate social behavior, are essential to thriving in nature.

Not all of the information posted on the internet is accurate, and one must be careful about the source from which the information is taken. If you come across a website that gives formulas or step-by-step directions on caring for a wild animal: BEWARE! Professional organizations do not give out that kind of assistance, and the information given is often wrong, deficient and dangerous.

It's also a sad discovery when a person rescues a baby animal that didn't need help. The "rescue" itself may have been the only thing that put its life in peril. If the person finding the animal had had immediate information at hand, he or she may have made better choices leading to freedom for the animal and enlightenment for the finder. Time is of the essence! Baby animals kidnapped for short periods of time can be successfully returned to the parent, den, or nest.

The purpose of this book is to supply you with accurate and immediate direction before you do anything dangerous or unnecessary. The recommendations I give will not only help you get the best possible care for the animal but will also have your safety in mind.

I've tried to present the information in an easy, orderly fashion so that you can find exactly what you need to know when you need it. Although reading through the many sections will help you understand the concepts behind wildlife rescue, the magic of this book lies in the dichotomous keys that begin on page 1. Through a series of questions and answers, these charts will walk you through many common backyard wildlife scenarios and point you to the best information for your situation.

If you were hoping for a step-by-step guide on how to rehabilitate wildlife yourself or on how to raise a baby animal, this book may be a disappointment. It is my firm belief that the science of rehabilitation should be left to licensed and trained individuals who have the knowledge, supplies, and veterinary support to offer that wild animal its very best chance for survival. Although many people have successfully raised baby bunnies on homemade formulas, the future health and survival of all wild creatures depends on their having the best in nutrition, habitat enrichment, and reintroduction into the wild.

All states have laws governing the possession of some or all wildlife. These laws are in place to protect both the animals and the public. Wildlife rehabilitators are licensed by state and federal agencies, or both, and have the resources available to offer the very best to wildlife in distress.

Remember: animals have not read our books on how they are supposed to behave. Every situation is different and poses unforeseen problems and dangers. For you to properly prepare in advance, I would strongly suggest that you start by finding your closest wildlife rehabilitators and keeping their numbers at home, in your car, and in your cell phone.

If you are interested in working with wildlife, you might consider volunteering with your local rehabilitator or becoming one yourself. Again, the best place to start is with the licensed rehabilitator near you.

You can find resources for locating wildlife rehabilitators on page 120.

THANK YOU FOR CARING ABOUT WILD ANIMALS.

DICHOTOMOUS KEYS

The dichotomous keys -- or flow charts -- for birds and mammals on the following pages are easy to follow. Directions are listed in the key itself, or for more thorough instructions, you will be directed to another section of the book. For this reason, it would be beneficial to have a bookmark on hand to mark your place.

We have tried to include as many common scenarios as possible, but no book can cover everything. Given the situation, you may need to talk directly with a rehabilitator or to use your own judgment. Remember, animals have not read our books on how they are supposed to behave, and you may witness animal behavior that no one could have predicted. Expect the unexpected. You are dealing with a wild animal, and unpredictability is the only firm rule.

Remember: keep your safety and the animal's safety foremost in your mind.

BIRDS

B1. Is this

A. an adult? (go to B2)

B. a nestling? (sparse or no feathers or covered with down) (go to B10)

C. a fledgling? (has feathers, but often the tail feathers are shorter than an adult's) (go to B33)

B2. Has this bird been captured?

A. Yes (go to B3)

B. No (go to B4)

C. It is trapped in a building. (go to page 39)

B3. Because of its ability to escape, an adult bird in hand is in distress and needs help. Be prepared to transport the bird to a wildlife rehabilitator.

- For more information on containment and transportation, see page 85.
- To find a rehabilitator near you, go to page 120.

B4. Is the bird injured or sick? Are you sure?

A. Yes (go to B5)

B. No, but it's friendly and approaching people. (go to B9)

C. It's attacking my house, windows, or people. (go to page 113)

D. I'm not sure. Help me decide. (go to B8)

B5. Are you willing to safely capture and transport the bird to a rehabilitator?

A. Yes (go to B6)

B. No (go to B7)

B6. Thank you for being willing to go the extra mile for this animal. Please be prepared to transport the bird to a wildlife rehabilitator.

- For more information on safe capture, see page 68.
- For more information on containment and transportation, see page 85.
- To find a rehabilitator near you, go to page 120.

B7. Unfortunately, there is probably not much help available if you or someone else is not willing to get involved. Most rehabilitators are not in the position to be out capturing animals. Will you reconsider?

A. Yes, give me the capture directions. (go to B6)

B. No

- To understand why these services are not commonly available, see page 119.
- To locate a rehabilitator on the off chance that he or she can arrange a capture and transport, go to page 120.

B8. Is this bird in distress? The following are signs of a bird in distress (for more details, see page 37):

Bleeding
Unconsciousness
Abnormal use or position of limb(s)
Odd head position
Maggots
Was in a cat's or dog's mouth
Drainage from the eyes
Behaving abnormally
Cold and lethargic
Heat exhaustion and exposure
Inability to escape

A. Yes, this bird appears to be in distress. (go to B8)

B. No, this bird does not appear to be in distress. (go to B39)

B9. A friendly bird may be an imprint ("tame" as a result of being hand-raised). This is often seen with waterfowl. It needs to be evaluated. Contact a rehabilitator.

- To better understand imprinting, see page 102.
- To find a rehabilitator, see page 120.

B10. Is this baby bird sick, injured, or has it already suffered from extreme exposure (heat or cold)?

A. Yes, help me locate a rehabilitator quickly!!! (go to page 120)

B. No (go to B11)

B11. What type of bird is it?

A. Fishing bird (herons, egrets, loons, etc.) (go to B30)

B. Raptor (go to B12)

C. Waterfowl (ducks and geese) (go to B26)

D. Songbird (small and helpless) (go to B31)

E. Ground bird (pheasant and quail) (go to B26)

F. I don't know. Help me decide. (go to B35)

B12. Is this a hawk (also falcons), owl or vulture?

A. Hawk (also falcons) (go to B13)

B. Owl (go to B16)

C. Vulture (go to B21)

D. I don't know. Help me decide. (go to B25)

B13. What is the situation with this young hawk?

A. Mother is known to be dead (go to page 120)

B. Nest fell or nest removed (go to B14)

C. In an inappropriate or dangerous location (go to B15)

D. Alone, but in a safe location (go to B15)

B14. Are the hawk's parents nearby?

A. Yes (go to B17)

B. No (go to B15)

B15. If the hawk's parents are in the area, leave it alone. Your definition of an inappropriate location may be different from that of the parents who chose this nesting site. Carefully consider the location and how you may be able to reunite the family. If you have seen the parents and you can safely do so, move the baby into a more secluded or safer place in that same area.

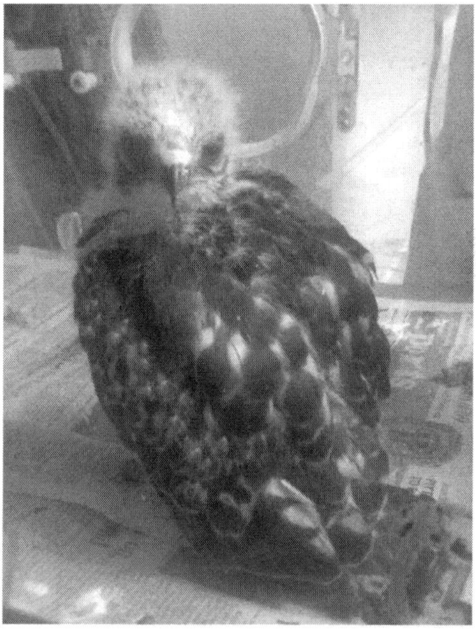

A baby hawk in the middle of a busy street may be able to be moved to the surrounding forest.

A baby hawk in the middle of an urban neighborhood may have fallen from a building. If it is not injured and you know the nesting area or the building from which it came, perhaps the bird can be returned to the nest. If the location is such that it is far too dangerous for the bird and too dangerous for you to reach a safe area, then call a rehabilitator (go to page 120).

If you do attempt to reunite the family, monitor the baby for a few days. If it remains strong and healthy, the parents are caring for it. If it becomes weakened, then call a rehabilitator (go to page 120).

B16. Owls come in a wide variety of sizes, and adults of small species are often mistaken for babies.

An adult owl will be fully feathered with no down. A baby owl will have thick down, while a fledgling owl will have both down and new feather growth.

Babies are typically born in the early-to-mid spring and fledge before summer. If it is any other time of year, please start over and consider this to be an adult owl.

Adult screech owls are only six inches tall and the size of a softball and are often misidentified as baby great horned owls. Compare the two pictures below to identify the owl you have encountered.

A. This is a baby owl. (go to B18)

B. These are small adult owls. (return to B1)

B17. Monitor the baby for a few days. If it remains strong and healthy, the parents are caring for it. If it becomes weakened, then call a rehabilitator (go to page 120).

B18. What is the situation with this young owl?

A. Parents are known to be dead (go to page 120)

B. Nest fell or nest removed (go to B19)

C. Inappropriate location (go to B20)

D. On ground alone (go to B20)

B19. If the parents are in the area, leave it alone. Owls often exit the nest very early; therefore, it's natural for parents to tend to baby owls on the ground.

If this is a small species of owl that may easily fall to predation, you can place the baby high up in a tree for protection.

If this is a larger species, such as a great horned owl, and the baby has developed beyond being a helpless hatchling, leave it where it is. It can defend itself from most predators.

Monitor the family for a few days to make sure the parents don't abandon the baby because of the nest accident. If it remains strong and healthy, the parents are caring for it. If it becomes weakened, then call a rehabilitator (go to page 120).

B20. Large owls, such as great horned owls, leave the nest weeks before they can fly. The parents continue tending to them. Once they begin to develop feathers, they are able to defend themselves against common predators such as cats. Large dogs, however, may pose a threat. If the owls are still down-covered, they may not have yet developed enough to protect themselves, and they should be moved up into a nearby tree.

Great horned owl babies are often found on low branches, logs, or even on the ground.

Smaller species of owls, such as screech owls, cannot defend themselves and, if they cannot yet fly, should be placed up in a tree out of harm's way.

Some species, such as the short-eared and snowy owls, nest directly on the ground.

Your definition of an inappropriate location may be different from that of the parents who chose this nesting site. Carefully consider the location and how you may be able to reunite the family. Usually, baby owls should be just left alone.

If you haven't seen the parents and you can safely do so, move the baby into a more secluded or safer place in that same area.

A baby owl in the middle of a busy street may be able to be moved to the surrounding forest.

A baby owl in the middle of a busy urban neighborhood is in grave danger. If it is not injured and you know the nesting area (probably a local group of conifer trees), perhaps the bird can be returned to the nesting area. If the location is such that it is far too dangerous for the bird, then call a rehabilitator (go to page 120).

Monitor the owlet for a few days. If it remains strong and healthy, the parents are caring for it. If it becomes weakened, then call a rehabilitator (go to page 120).

B21. People often mistake baby pigeons for baby vultures. Here's how to tell the difference:

A. Pigeons are the size of a softball, or smaller, and have sparse down that looks like it was burned (go to B22).

Baby pigeons (squabs)

B. Vultures have thick reddish or white down. Turkey vultures have a "peep sight" at the nares (nostrils) (go to B23).

A juvenile vulture

The "peep sight" of a turkey vulture's nares

B22. Pigeons nest just about anywhere. There are usually two babies, and there might be no nest at all. They can be found on ledges, in old nests, and even on the ground under a bush. Mothers do not tend to their babies often, feeding them only two to four times a day. If the baby is not injured, leave it alone.

B23. Vultures do not build nests, and babies are often found alone on rock ledges and in caves. In rural areas, barns and silos may appear to be caves. In urban areas, abandoned warehouses, factories, and other large buildings with broken windows could also be considered a cave to a nesting vulture. These are all natural and should not be disturbed.

A baby vulture found in someone's backyard or hopping down the street is not normal and needs help (go to page 120).

B24. If the babies can be captured, place them in a tall, slim box (upright vacuum-cleaner type) and set the box near the parents. Watch from a distance. The sound of the babies should attract the parents. Often the mother will come and knock over the box and take the baby(ies) with her. If she doesn't respond, the babies are already contained; and you can take them to a rehabilitator.

- To find a rehabilitator, go to page 120.

B25. All baby raptors are covered with a thick down. Use this guide to identify your bird:

A. Hawks (also falcons) have curved beaks and strong feet that are completely bare (go to B13).

B. Owls have curved beaks and strong feet that are completely covered in down (go to B16).

C. Vultures have thick reddish or white down. Turkey vultures have a "peep sight" at the nares (nostrils) (go to B23).

D. Baby pigeons are often confused with raptors (go to B22).

E. Grouse and chickens are often confused with raptors. They have hefty feet with a small rear toe (go to B26).

B26. What is the situation with the waterfowl or ground bird?

A. Mother is known to be dead (go to page120)

B. Alone with no parent (go to B27)

C. Trapped in a drain or other obstacle (go to B29)

B27. Do you know the location of the mother?

A. Yes (go to B24)

B. No (go to B28)

B28. Baby ducks, geese, and ground birds such as pheasant, quail, and turkey need their parents at all times. They are NEVER left alone by their parents. Please take this baby to a wildlife rehabilitator who can raise it or who may be able to introduce it to a surrogate family of the same species.

- To find a rehabilitator go to page 120.

B29. Each situation is different and beyond this key. As a general guide:

If the mother can be captured, her calls will attract the babies toward a net, box, or corral.

If the babies can be captured, place them in a tall, slim box (like one an upright vacuum cleaner would come in) and set the box near the parents. Watch from a distance.

The sound of the babies should attract the parents. Often the mother will come and knock over the box and take the babies with her. If she doesn't respond, the babies are already contained, and you can take them to a rehabilitator.

- To find a rehabilitator go to page 120.

B30. ***DANGER -- Please read the section on fishing birds BEFORE approaching any babies or adults. See page 76.***

Because herons and egrets build their nests so very high up in the trees, returning a baby to its nest is nearly impossible. Nests are guarded almost all the time until the babies are about a month old.

If the baby has feathers and appears otherwise healthy and uninjured, monitor the baby for a few days. If it remains strong and healthy, the parents are caring for it. If it becomes weakened, then call a rehabilitator.

If the baby is very young with down, it probably should be taken directly to a rehabilitator.

- To find a rehabilitator, go to page 120.

B31. What is the situation with the baby songbird?

- **A.** Mother is known to be dead. (go to page 120)
- **B.** Nest fell or nest removed. Tree cut down. (go to B32)
- **C.** On the ground. Out of nest. Inappropriate location. (go to B34)
- **D.** Note on Mourning Doves: does your baby look like this? (go to B37)

B32. You can make a new nest for the baby bird, and the parents should begin caring for it again.

- For instructions on returning babies to nests or how to rebuild nests, see page 45.
- To find a rehabilitator, go to page 120.

B33. Is this bird injured? Are you sure? Flightlessness doesn't always mean a bird is injured.

A. Yes. This bird is injured. (go to page 120)

B. I'm not sure if it's injured or not. Help me decide. (go to B38)

C. It's hopping around but can't fly. (go to B36)

B34. If the baby bird is not injured, has not suffered from exposure, and you know where the nest is (and can reach it), place the baby back in the nest. It is a fallacy that touching a wild baby will cause the mother to reject or kill it.

A. If the baby is dehydrated, cold and lethargic, or has been exposed to the sun and is too hot, it needs to see a rehabilitator immediately (go to page 120).

B. If you generally know where the baby came from, but you cannot find or reach the actual nest, go to page 69.

C. To locate a rehabilitator now, just in case, go to page 120.

B35. Which of the following best describes this bird?

A. Thick down with a curved, sharp beak and strong feet (go to B25)

B. Thick down, walking on its own, webbed feet (go to B26)

C. Thick down, walking on its own, slim toes (go to B26)

D. Naked or with sparse down, helpless. Might be opening its mouth begging for food (go to B31)

B36. Fledglings go through a period when they are just learning to fly. Depending on the species, it can take several hours or several days for them to get off the ground. Once they learn to fly, the parents gather them together and begin teaching them the survival skills they need, such as how to find food.

People often find fledgling birds temporarily stranded in a yard or on a porch and think they need help. Unable to fly, the fledglings become prey to pet dogs and cats.

This is an important transition time for these birds, and it should not be interrupted. Birds brought to rehab at this age often fail. They are not old enough to feed themselves, but they know we are not their parents and resist hand-feeding. Force-feeding places them under great stress, and they will often die.

If they are uninjured, stranded fledglings can be moved to a safer location nearby. Moving them to a nearby tree limb or herding them to a sheltered area is all the "rescuing" they need.

B37. Mourning Doves do not build their own nests. They often nest directly on the ground under a low bush. They will also nest in old bird nests, flower pots---just about anywhere. There are usually two babies to a nest. Unlike other songbirds, the parents do not feed them often and may only visit them for feeding several times each day.

It is easy to determine if a nestling dove has been recently fed by the parents. In the picture below, the dove on the right has been recently fed and has a swollen neck area. The dove on the left has an empty crop. A baby dove can be checked periodically to see if the crop area enlarges. If it does, the parents are feeding it.

If a baby dove is not injured, then leave it alone. It is fine, and the parents are caring for it.

Young fledgling and pre-fledgling doves look much like the adults. You can easily tell the difference by the shape of the tail. Adults have a sharply pointed tail, whereas a juvenile's tail is rounded.

Young doves are easily approached and should be left alone except when they have an obvious injury.

B38. The following are signs of a bird in distress. (For more details, see page 63.)

Bleeding
Unconsciousness
Abnormal use or position of limb(s)
Odd head position
Maggots
Was in a cat's or dog's mouth
Drainage from the eyes
Behaving abnormally
Cold and lethargic
Heat exhaustion and exposure

Is this bird in distress?

A. Yes

- To find a rehabilitator, go to page 120.

B. No, it appears that there is nothing wrong (go to B36)

B39. Although it appears that nothing is wrong, you may want to monitor the situation for a day or so.

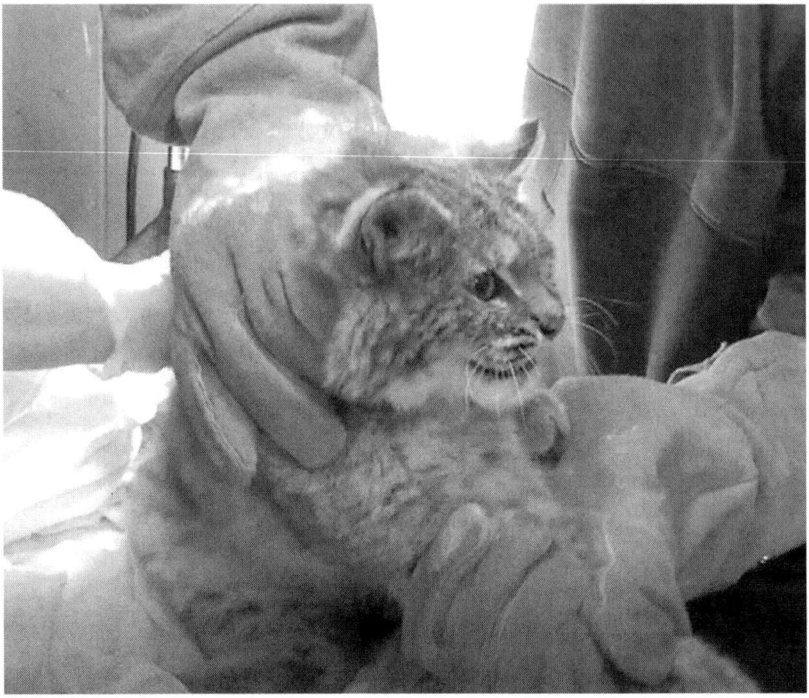

MAMMALS

Before we begin the mammal section, let's make sure there are no people in danger of exposure to rabies.

M1. Was anyone bitten or scratched, or did saliva from the animal come in contact with an open cut or mucous membrane such as the eyes? Have you been caring for this animal for a day or more, feeding it or handling dishes?

A. No (go to M3)

B. Yes (go to M2)

C. Rabies does not exist in this area. (go to M3)

- For more information on rabies, go to page 99.

M2. Although any warm-blooded animal can contract rabies, some species, (such as raccoons, skunks, and bats) are more prone to transmitting the virus.

A. If you (or someone else) have had a possible exposure, call you family physician, hospital emergency room, or your state's department of health for information on your health and how to proceed.

- For more information on rabies, go to page 99.

B. Continue with the mammal section (go to M3).

M3. Is this

A. an adult? (go to M4)

B. a juvenile? (eyes open but still dependent on parents) (go to M19)

C. an infant? (eyes closed, unable to walk) (go to M11)

M4. What is the situation with this adult mammal?

- **A.** Animal is sick or injured, but it has not been captured. (go to M5)
- **B.** Animal is sick or injured, and it has been captured. (go to page 85)
- **C.** Animal is acting friendly (or aggressively), and it is approaching people or pets. (go to M10)
- **D.** Animal is acting abnormally or "hanging out" (nocturnal animal out during the day). (go to M9)
- **E.** I'm not sure. Help me decide. (go to M8)
- **F.** Animal is a nuisance, and I want it removed. (go to page 111)

M5. Most rehabilitators are volunteers and do not have the ability to go out and capture animals. Are you willing to safely capture and transport the animal to a rehabilitator?

- **A.** Yes. Give me safe capture instructions. (go to M6)
- **B.** No (go to M7)
- **C.** This animal is too dangerous because of its size or aggressive behavior. (go to Page 120)

M6. Only attempt to capture the animal if you can safely do so.

- For more information on specific capture instructions, read "Injured Wildlife 101" on page 31 and "Capture" on page 68.
- To find a rehabilitator, go to page 120.

M7. Unfortunately, there is probably not much help available if you or someone else is unwilling to get involved. Will you reconsider?

- **A.** Yes. Give me safe capture instructions. (go to M6)
- To understand why these services are not commonly available, see page 119.
- To find a rehabilitator, go to page 120.

M8. The following are signs of an animal in distress. (For more details, see page 37.)

Bleeding
Unconsciousness
Abnormal use or position of limb(s)
Odd head position
Maggots
Was in a cat's or dog's mouth
Drainage from the eyes
Behaving abnormally
Cold and lethargic
Heat exhaustion and exposure
Inability to escape

Is this animal in distress?

A. Yes (go to M5)
B. No (go to M33)

M9. A nocturnal animal out during the day may or may not be a problem. If a mother has babies in the den, she may be hunting. Animals can also be routed from their den accidentally and become disoriented until they find a new place.

If the animal does not appear injured, give it a day or two for reorientation. The problem may rectify itself naturally.

A. Animal is acting friendly (or aggressively) and is approaching people or pets. (go to M10)

- To find a rehabilitator, go to page 120.

M10. This is a very dangerous situation that can have many causes, including head injury, imprinting, and disease (including rabies).

Do not approach this animal! Keep pets and children away! Call a rehabilitator immediately!

- For more on imprinting, see page 102.
- For more on rabies, see page 99.
- To find a rehabilitator, see page 120.

M11. Is this infant animal sick, injured, or has it already suffered from extreme exposure (heat or cold)?

- **A.** No (go to M12)
- **B.** Yes. Help me locate a rehabilitator quickly!
- To find a rehabilitator, go to page 120.

M12. It is often difficult to determine whether a baby animal needs help, should simply be left alone to be whisked away by a parent, or just moved to a safer place. No one can raise a wild baby better than the parent. Great care must be taken in deciding whether to interfere.

- **A.** Deer (go to M23)
- **B.** Cottontail rabbit (go to M13)
- **C.** Opossum (go to page 64)
- **D.** Infant of another species (go to M24)

M13. What is the problem with this bunny?

- **A.** Possibly abandoned or orphaned (go to page 51)
- **B.** Baby not in nest and location of nest is unknown (go to Page 120)
- **C.** Nest was moved or destroyed by construction, gardening, etc. (go to M18)
- **D.** Lawn mower accident (go to M17)
- **E.** Brought home by children (go to M14)
- **F.** Nest in a public area and known to many children (go to M16)
- **G.** Brought home by pet (go to M15)
- **H.** Nest was discovered or touched (go to M14)

M14. Baby bunnies can be returned to the nest if the following criteria are met:

Babies are uninjured.

You have not had them in your possession for more than one day.

You have not fed them any type of milk replacers, formulas, or other types of food.

You know the location of the nest.

A. We do not meet these criteria. Help me find a rehabilitator (go to page 120).

B. We meet these criteria. Give us the instructions for proper reintroduction to the nest and how to test if the mother returns (go to page 51).

M15. Dogs, and especially cats, can carry the bacteria *Pasteurella,* which is highly infectious to wild animals. If the animal was attacked or carried by a pet, it will need a regimen of antibiotics to prevent infection.

A. Any baby animal that was in a cat's or dog's mouth should be taken to a wildlife rehabilitator.

- To find a rehabilitator, go to page 120.

M16. People and pets should be kept away from the nest for 10 to 14 days. If this is impossible or if you have no control over the property, take the babies to a wildlife rehabilitator right away.

A. If children or pets can be kept away, go to M14.

- To find a rehabilitator, go to page 120.

M17. If some babies were injured or killed but others are untouched, blood from the injured babies will probably attract flies. These flies will lay eggs, and the hatching maggots will consume all of the babies. All the babies should be taken to a rehabilitator.

If all the babies are unharmed, restore the nest and test to make sure the mother returns.

A. For instructions on testing the nest for the mother's return, go to page 54.

- To find a rehabilitator, go to page 120.

M18. Heavy construction often will cause abandonment of the nesting area. Gardening or accidental disturbance of the nest may not. Can the nest be rebuilt in the exact same location?

A. No (go to page 120)

B. Yes (go to page 51)

M19. Is this young animal sick or injured?

A. Yes, this animal is injured (go to page 120).

B. No (go to M20)

C. I'm not sure if it's injured or not. Help me decide. (go to M21)

M20. It is often not easy to determine whether a baby animal needs your help, simply needs to be left alone to be whisked away by a parent, or just moved to a safer place. No one can raise a wild baby better than the parent, so great care must be taken in deciding whether to interfere in that life.

A. Deer (go to M23)

B. Cottontail rabbit (go to M22)

C. Opossum (go to 64)

D. Infant of another species (go to M24)

M21. The following are signs of a baby mammal in distress. (For more details, see page 37.)

Bleeding
Unconsciousness
Abnormal use or position of limb(s)
Odd head position
Maggots
Was in a cat's or dog's mouth
Drainage from the eyes
Behaving abnormally
Cold and lethargic
Heat exhaustion and exposure

Is this animal in distress?

A. Yes (go to page 120)

B. No (go to M20)

M22. Is this bunny over four inches long, hopping, and able to make its ears stand up?

A. No, this bunny is younger than that. (go to M13)

B. Yes, that describes this bunny. (go to page 56)

C. This bunny is over four inches long, but it is in an unsafe location. (go to page 56)

At five inches long, this bunny is old enough to care for itself.

M23. People often find fawns and think that they are orphaned or abandoned. The fawn will be seen day after day, in the exact same place, alone.

Was this fawn found with its dead mother or has it been alone in an area?

A. This fawn is approaching people and has been crying loudly for the entire day. (go to page 61)

B. This fawn is a true orphan as it was found with its dead mother. (go to page 63)

C. There is no mother in the area. The fawn is alone. (go to page 58)

M24. What is the situation?

A. Found alone (go to M30)

B. Nest disturbed/animals touched (go to M26)

C. Mother is known to be dead (go to page 120)

D. Nest destroyed/tree cut down (go to M27)

E. Exposed to the elements (go to M29)

M25. Place the babies under shelter and leave them alone in the area for a few hours (nocturnal animals need to be left overnight). Check back in a few hours. If they have not been moved by the mother, call a rehabilitator.

- To find a rehabilitator, go to page 120.

M26. It is commonly believed that touching a baby animal will cause the mother to reject or kill it. This is an "old wives' tale" and is not true. Babies can be returned to the nest if these criteria are met:

1. Babies are uninjured.
2. You have not had them in your possession for more than one day.
3. You have not fed them any type of milk replacers, formulas, or other types of food.
4. You know the location of the nest.

A. We meet these criteria. (go to M32)
B. We do not meet these criteria. Help me find a rehabilitator.

- To find a rehabilitator, go to page 120.

M27. Do you know the location of the den or nest?
A. Yes (go to M32)
B. No (go to M25)

M28. Babies can be returned to the nest if these criteria are met:

1. Babies are uninjured.
2. They were found within the last 24 hours.
3. You have not fed them any type of milk replacers, formulas, or other types of food.
4. You know the location of the nest.

A. We meet these criteria. (go to M32)
B. We do not meet these criteria. Help me find a rehabilitator.

- To find a rehabilitator, go to page 120.

M29. Has the baby's health been compromised because of exposure? (too hot or too cold?)

A. Yes (go to page 120)

B. No (go to M27)

M30. Is the baby sick or injured? Is "being alone" its only problem? It is normal to find a healthy baby with no sign of the parents. The parents may be out searching for food or even watching from a distance. Some animals do not utilize dens, and babies can be found out in the open.

A. I don't know if it's injured. (go to M31)

B. It doesn't appear to be injured. (go to M28)

C. It's injured. (go to page 120)

M31. The following are signs of a baby mammal in distress. (For more details, see page 31.)

Bleeding
Unconsciousness
Abnormal use or position of limb(s)
Odd head position
Maggots
Was in a cat's or dog's mouth
Drainage from the eyes
Behaving abnormally
Cold and lethargic
Heat exhaustion and exposure

Is this animal in distress?

A. Yes (go to page 120)

B. No (go to M30)

M32. Please return the babies to their den.

M33. Although it appears that nothing is wrong, you may want to monitor the situation for a day or so.

The initial encounter with an injured animal can be heartbreaking. Human instinct tells us to help at all cost; but the results of a sudden, unplanned action can be very damaging for the animal and for you.

Stop, look around, and plan every action beforehand. If there are other people around, talk to them and work together. Create a plan and move from there.

Before taking any action, call for advice if you can. This is where having your local wildlife rehabilitator's number saved in your cell phone comes in handy. Keep a safe distance from the animal and relay any details you can about the species, size, and type of injury. Remember the location and the surrounding scene. Also, describe any obvious injuries that you observe.

> ***If you need to capture the animal, think SAFETY first: YOUR SAFETY as well as the ANIMAL'S SAFETY.***

Forget about the "Kamikaze-style" of animal capture where the person rushes in with reckless abandon as is often seen on television today. Such high-action scenes are probably well planned out before the camera starts rolling, and the drama is for ratings, not conservation.

Take a step back and review the situation carefully. As you scan the area, observe the animal before approaching it. In some cases, binoculars can be used to examine the animal before entering its danger zone.

Taking a short time to assess the situation and examining the animal before approaching it, eliminates surprises and unnecessary injury to you, the bystanders, and the animal. Look for anything that can give clues as to what happened. Seek out escape routes that the animal may take and the dangers that await it there such as traffic, dogs, cliffs, and water.

PURSUIT

Animals that are difficult to approach can often be chased to an enclosed area such as a fenced yard, barn, or barnyard. Bystanders can help direct an animal to a confined location, thus trapping the animal.

On the other hand, pursuing an animal that is fleeing from you is not always a good idea. It is highly unlikely that you will be able to outrun the animal, and you could be seriously injured if you trip or fall. As humans, we consider ourselves the most intelligent of species, and you must "outthink" the animal so that you can capture it before it has a chance to escape. This is why surveying the area and having a capture plan is so important.

If an animal has escaped, and it's obvious that capture attempts will be futile, STOP! If the animal can't be captured, it may not need help. Keep an eye out for the animal for several days. If its condition deteriorates, capture may be attempted later.

Before doing anything, ask yourself if you are truly prepared to help this animal.

Is it dangerous? Do you have the mobility and strength to control it without getting hurt?

Do you have a box, carrier, or other type of container in which to confine it? Do you have safety equipment such as gloves and eye protection?

Injured adult animals can present themselves in varying degrees of distress: from slightly injured and trying to escape, to self-defensive, to completely unaware and possibly unconscious. Do not allow an animal's lack of responsiveness result in your letting your guard down. An animal can awaken suddenly and strike out. Many species will feign sleep as a way of protecting themselves. No matter what the degree of its injury, treat that animal as if it is the most dangerous creature on the planet.

SAFETY

I mentioned earlier that there are risks to your health and safety when rescuing wildlife. This warning should not be taken lightly! Protecting yourself from bites and scratches is a concern, but handling an animal in a way that protects you from exposure to parasites and disease is just as important.

Different animals attack differently, and the effects can be quite damaging. Most people are aware of the danger of claws and teeth from a mammal, but birds can also be very dangerous.

A heron or loon will strike out with its long, pointed beak, aiming for the hands and face. A single strike to an eye can cause serious, permanent injury to (or the loss of) that eye, and, in theory, a well-placed strike could kill a person.

Although its bite can be very painful, a raptor's primary weapon is its feet. The raptor foot, designed for capturing prey, is equipped with long, sharp talons that can be driven deep into the skin -- piercing nerves, tendons, and blood vessels. The foot pressure is extremely strong for the bird's size, and the tendons keep the foot closed -- making the foot of even a small raptor, such as a screech owl or an American kestrel, difficult to remove. A red-tailed hawk can deliver up to five hundred pounds of pressure per square inch, and a great horned owl can deliver up to THREE times that amount of pressure!

Geese, although a prey species that is large but seemingly unequipped for battle, can do great harm. Although their feet are harmless and their beak can only cause a deep bruise, their wings are formidable weapons. At the wrist joint of the wing is a protruding bone called the *alula*. It is hard and sharp, and with the driving force of the powerful wing behind it, can act as a barbed club hitting a person in the face and head.

Traumatic injury is not the only danger to a person rescuing a wild animal. Zoonotic diseases, parasites, and infection can cause long-term problems that range from mild irritations to death.

Rabies is a fatal disease common in many areas. Any warm-blooded animal can contract the virus, and prevention from exposure needs to be the first concern when dealing with mammals. Frequently contracted through a bite or scratch from an affected animal, rabies can also be contracted by getting infected saliva into an open scratch, cut, sore, or by it's coming into contact with mucous membranes. For more on rabies, see page 99.

Infections from bites can also cause serious conditions even if the animal does not have an active disease. Many animals carry bacteria in their mouths and on their claws that are benign to them, but highly infectious to people. Localized infection may occur, but systemic infection is also a danger. Many years ago, I had a very painful swelling of numerous lymph nodes that turned out to be a *Pasteurella* infection from a bite that I had received several weeks before. Although the initial wound had healed, the bacteria found a weak part of my body's systems in which to grow. If left untreated, such an infection can cause damage to the body's organs, including permanent heart damage.

Another danger when handling wild animals is exposure to parasites. Although there are many, the most noted example is *Baylisascaris* (Bay-liss-ass-kuh-ris) procyonis, or raccoon roundworm. This parasite doesn't seem to cause much harm in its intended host, the raccoon, but it can cause severe medical problems when ingested by the wrong host. When ingested by humans, the parasite leaves the digestive tract and circulates through the body by way of the bloodstream, often getting lodged in the smallest of blood vessels, where it becomes a cyst. Depending on the location, the parasite can cause skin irritations or eye and brain damage in humans. If the blood vessels of the eyes or brain are involved, blindness and even death can result. The same happens in other "unintended" hosts such as dogs and cats.

These are only a few examples of the most common dangers of handling wildlife. As you can see, exposure for even a short time can be costly. If you care for and house an animal for any period of time, the threat is heightened, and the danger is spread to other family members as well as to pets.

Now that I have outlined a few of the dangers of handling wild animals and stressed the importance of safety (and if I haven't scared you completely away from saving that creature in need), it's time to talk about helping that animal.

THE ANIMAL'S POINT OF VIEW

It doesn't matter how much you love animals or how noble your intentions are; in the animal's mind, you are the enemy. We often have people who see an animal suddenly calm down once it's captured and think, "It knows I'm trying to help it." That notion may be romantic, but it is rarely accurate.

Most animals recognize predators instinctively by the location of their eyes. Most prey species have eyes on the sides of their heads, which gives them extended peripheral vision; predators' eyes are on the fronts of their faces, which gives them good depth perception. To an animal, you have the eyes of a predator. If you eat meat, you smell like a predator. If you smile caringly at the animal, you are baring your teeth. From the animal's perspective, it has just lost the life-and-death struggle of predator and prey and is about to become your lunch.

Now, add to this the fact that the animal is incapacitated. Wildlife that is sick, injured, or orphaned is already experiencing a great deal of stress. It may be suffering from dehydration, starvation, blood loss, and injury. It will probably be in moderate to severe pain. It definitely will be fearful. The animal doesn't want to be rescued. If given the chance, it would hide in a quiet place and recover or die on its own.

I'm not telling you these things to dissuade you from helping that wild animal but to help you understand the need for minimal handling. The steps you take to help this animal need to include the least amount of handling and movement to reduce the amount of stress to the animal and minimize the danger to you.

DOES THIS ANIMAL TRULY NEED HELP?

Because rescuing an animal does involve danger to you and the animal, your very first question should be, "Does this animal really need help?"

With adult animals, it is relatively easy to determine whether the animal needs help. Our rule of thumb is "If you can catch it, it's in trouble!"

Juvenile and baby animals are another matter. If there is no obvious injury, perhaps the animal needs only to be left alone or to be moved to a safe location until its mother returns to retrieve it.

If you are unsure about an animal's need for rescue, using the dichotomous keys beginning on page 1 will help you determine the proper steps to take.

ADULT ANIMAL EMERGENCIES

Every situation is different, and no two animals will act the same even if they have the same condition or injury. There are, however, typical signs of distress evident much of the time, and knowing these can help determine if an animal is truly in need of help.

With adult animals, often the most obvious sign is the inability to escape. No self-respecting adult animal will allow you to approach it. If it can't or won't avoid your approach, there's a problem.

SIGNS OF DISTRESS

The following signs are considered true emergencies with adult animals:

Inability to escape is usually the first sign that an animal is in trouble. Any healthy ADULT animal will not allow itself to be captured or handled.

Bleeding is an immediate, life-threatening condition. If possible, every effort should be made to stop the bleeding at the scene. See the "Alleviate Life-Threatening Conditions" section for "Bleeding" (page 94).

Unconsciousness is an obvious emergency needing immediate medical attention. Always use caution, however, even when handling an unconscious animal. It can recover quite suddenly; and some animals, such as opossums and screech owls, will feign death when threatened or stressed. Remember, even a seemingly incapacitated animal can be potentially dangerous.

Abnormal use or position of limb(s) may indicate a fracture. Paralysis can be a sign of trauma or illness. Reduce the risk of further injury by placing padding or shredded newspaper in the container and packing the animal tightly enough to impede movement.

Odd head position can be the sign of a head or spinal trauma or disease.

Maggots and fly eggs may or may not accompany an open wound. Maggot eggs on fur or feathers look like cream or yellowish, fuzzy dandruff. This is a sure sign that the animal is in serious trouble. If left untreated, maggots will burrow into wet tissue or openings in the skin and literally eat the animal alive.

An animal that was attacked or carried by a pet needs medical care. Dogs, and especially cats, carry bacteria in their mouths that are highly infectious to wild animals, particularly birds and rabbits. The animal will need a regimen of antibiotics to prevent infection.

Drainage from eyes or nose is an indication of illness that needs medical attention. Even if the illness is not contagious or immediately life-threatening, it will impede an animal's ability to hunt or to escape predation.

Animals behaving abnormally need to be handled with extreme caution. Rabid animals will often act friendly, as will animals imprinted on humans. Both situations present a great risk to you and anyone assisting you. See the sections on "Rabies" (page 99) and on "Imprinting" (page 102).

Cold and lethargic animals are suffering from hypothermia. They are usually in shock and, if not treated immediately, may die suddenly. See the section on "Hypothermia" (page 95.)

Heat exhaustion and exposure is another condition requiring immediate attention. See the section on "Hyperthermia" (page 95.)

ENTRAPMENT

Animals often become trapped in our man-made structures such as buildings, window wells, sewage drains, and fences.

Careful examination from a distance should determine whether the animal has suffered due to its confinement and needs extended care. If an animal is trapped but otherwise uninjured, it may need some assistance to help it escape.

It is often unnecessary to physically remove an adult animal; it only needs to be given an avenue of escape and a little "quiet time" to feel safe enough to leave.

BIRDS TRAPPED IN BUILDINGS

The most common situation involving entrapment is a hawk in a large building (such as a commercial structure), but any bird can get inside any building. The bird should first be encouraged to fly out; this can be accomplished by opening all the doors and windows and allowing the bird time to leave on its own.

If the bird refuses to leave; or if it is up high, and the doors are set much lower than the ceiling, it may need to be shown the route to exit. The trick is to use lighting. Daytime birds usually will not move in the dark. If they cannot see, they will not fly. Open the largest doors, which will allow light to come in, and turn out all the lights in the area. If there are windows that cannot be opened, cover these with cloth or cardboard to cut the light to a minimum. You may need to encourage the bird to leave the safety of its high perch by chasing it until it flies out. Loud noises and soft objects (such as wet sponges) thrown toward the bird will usually get it started.

If there are no doors or windows near the bird, or if the rescue is attempted at night, using the "lights out" technique can also work. For this approach, you need several people working together. One person stands by the power source to all lighting, while the others get ready for the capture. The bird is encouraged to move; and once it is in flight, the lights are turned off. Being unable to see, the bird should land on the floor where a blanket or box can be placed over it.

If the bird cannot be easily removed by this procedure, or if it has been trapped for several days, call a local rehabilitator to assist with this bird's return to health and freedom.

BATS IN BUILDINGS

Bats can enter a home by accidentally flying through an open door, window, chimney, or by working their way down from the attic.

A flying bat can be encouraged to leave at night by turning off all the indoor lights and shining a bright light into the doorway from outside. Headlights from a car work very well.

If the bat is clinging to a beam or a curtain, place a cup over the bat and slip a piece of cardboard under the cup, thus trapping the bat inside.

If outside temperatures allow, release the bat from the cup at the base of a tree so that it can crawl up into the tree and roost. If it is too cold for the bat to survive outdoors, call your local wildlife rehabilitator and transport the bat to them to winter-over. It will then be released in the spring.

Do not touch the bat with bare hands! Use lite leather gloves if you must handle the bat. If you are bitten, do not release the bat. It may need to be tested for rabies to ensure your health. If you are bitten, wake up with a bat in your bedroom, or if a bat was in a room with an unattended child or an unvaccinated pet, PLEASE read the section about rabies (page 99) and contact your local department of health immediately.

If bats are getting into your home on a regular basis, you may wish to contact an urban wildlife pest control person to provide bat exclusion for the building. Removing bats can be done humanely with one-way door systems that allow the bats to leave but do not allow re-entry. Once the bats are excluded, the entry points are sealed to keep any bats from returning.

ANIMAL HAS FALLEN INTO A PIT

Most animals will climb out of window wells and other holes if a blanket is secured from top to bottom. The best blankets to use for mammals are loosely woven so that they can get their claws into the fabric. Even skunks, the most common animal we see in this predicament, can climb so long as they can dig in their claws. Make sure the blanket is secured well enough to bear the animal's weight.

Leave the animal alone and keep children and pets away. It may take some time for the animal to feel safe enough to leave, and a nocturnal animal may wait until nighttime to make its escape.

ANIMAL'S HEAD STUCK IN HOLE

Freeing an animal whose head is stuck inside a hole or fence can be hazardous to both the animal and to the rescuer. A restrained animal will be in a panic and can fight its rescuer ferociously.

We've all seen photos and movies showing skunks wandering blindly with their heads stuck in yogurt containers.

It is possible that the animal will need medical care to correct dehydration and injuries. Although it may be tempting to free the animal and allow it to run off, releasing it immediately may not be the best thing for the animal.

If an animal's head is stuck in a movable container, such as a yogurt cup or a peanut butter jar, use the box-over method, as described on page 68, and transport the animal to a local rehabilitator or veterinarian for safe removal.

Sometimes an animal is trapped in a container that is not movable, such as when a skunk tries to enter a dumpster through the ground level drainage hole. Although its head and neck fit through while it's moving forward, the lay of the hair bunches up, which prevents its reversing back out of the hole.

Pulling the animal back through the hole is not recommended and can result in injuring the animal. For example, removing a sparrow whose head is stuck in a bluebird-box entry hole may seem like a simple enough task; but, according to Keith Galvin, Sr. of Galvin Wildlife Control, it often results in the sparrow's jaw being broken. The reason is that, although the sparrow appears to have its head stuck, it actually has lodged its lower beak in between two layers of wood while attempting to chip away at the hole to widen it.

The only way to humanely remove the bird is to use a screw driver to open the box by removing the lid or side panel and then gently prying the wood apart near the beak to free the lower jaw.

Deer caught with their bodies part way through a fence is another common type of entrapment. The deer will pass through the fence until the rails reach its hips, which are too wide to pass through the fence. The rib cage, which easily passed through the bars when the deer was moving forward, expands and keeps the animal from reversing back through the fence.

Extraction is possible; but it requires experienced intervention to ensure the safety of the rescuer and to reduce the risk of further injury to the animal. In this situation, emergency assistance should be called immediately. Stay with the animal and ensure that no one else attempts a rescue while you're waiting for help to arrive.

TURTLES

Wildlife rehabilitators have made great progress in saving injured and sick turtles. New methods of shell repair have been very successful, and the turtles respond well to antibiotic therapy as well as to treatment for parasites.

Healthy animals that are in a dangerous area, such as on a highway, can be moved a short walking distance to a safer location. Make sure to place the turtle toward the same direction in which it was originally headed, or it may retrace its steps back to where you picked it up.

Painted turtle with an ear abscess

Examine turtles for bleeding, cracked shells, and maggots. Examine the nostrils, eyes, and ears for any discharge or swelling. Any of these signs are life-threatening for the turtle.

Do not handle turtles more than absolutely necessary. Turtles carry bacteria that can make a person sick. YOUR bacteria can also make THEM sick, causing respiratory, eye, and ear infections.

Wash your hands with an anti-bacterial soap before eating, drinking, or smoking.

A NOTE ON THE EASTERN BOX TURTLE

The eastern box turtle population has dropped considerably over the past few decades. Research has found that box turtles may not have the ability to lure a mate through vocalizations, scents, or behaviors. Breeding relies solely on turtles seeing each other. Since mating is made possible only by one turtle accidentally meeting another, population density is very important. The sparser the population, the less chance there is for an accidental meeting and the less chance of a successful breeding. The situation spirals downward from there.

Eastern box turtle with an eye infection

It is also believed that adult box turtles do not survive long outside their normal, personal range. Evidence suggests that a box turtle that is moved too great a distance will not hibernate the next winter. One of the factors contributing to the decline of the eastern box turtle may be well-meaning people moving turtles to a "better" location for the turtles' safety.

When rescuing a box turtle, it is extremely important that you document exactly where it was found so that it can be returned to the exact area, where it may hibernate through the winter.

BABY ANIMAL EMERGENCIES

With adult wildlife, its inability to escape is a telltale sign of trouble. Baby animals may not have that ability, physically or mentally, so great care must be taken to ensure that a baby animal is truly in need of help. The kidnapping of baby animals is common and unnecessary. All babies do better with their natural parent than in rehabilitation, even if the location where they are growing up is questionable.

A FALLACY THAT KILLS

There is an "old wives' tale" that we frequently hear that is a major factor in baby animals being kidnapped: "If you touch a baby animal, the mother will reject or kill it." That is not true! **Mothers WILL NOT reject their babies because they were touched!**

Babies can be safely examined and returned to nests and dens with little risk of rejection. Every precaution should be taken, however, to avoid putting human scent on the babies or at the nest site so the nest is not detected by predators.

BABY BIRDS AND BIRD NESTS

One of the most common wildlife emergencies we see is baby birds that have fallen out of the nest, or the nest itself has fallen. This is an emergency requiring immediate attention, but one that often can be remedied quickly. Babies can be returned to nests, and entire nests can be repaired or replaced completely with great success and little disruption of the family.

If the baby is not injured and has not suffered extreme exposure from heat or cold, every attempt must be made to reunite the baby bird with its parents. No one can raise a baby bird like mom! The baby bird's chances of living a healthy, normal life are greatly increased by allowing nature to raise its own.

If a baby bird has fallen and the nest location is known (and can be reached), simply plop the baby back into the nest and walk away. Check back every few hours to make sure the bird remains in the nest. If it repeatedly falls, check the nest to see if it needs adjustment. A tilted nest will not hold babies well and can be straightened or secured.

Babies being repeatedly thrown from the nest by the parents may have a defect of which the parents are aware. They may not be willing to expend the energy to raise a baby that cannot survive. Such a bird can be taken to a wildlife rehabilitator.

Occasionally, sibling rivalry will cause a weaker baby to be thrown from the nest. In some cases, a parasitic bird species may be the culprit. Cowbirds, when hatched in a host nest, will push all the other birds out of the nest. This is nature at its finest, but it may be difficult to witness in your own backyard. In this case, consult your local rehabilitator for advice. They may take and raise the babies that have been victimized.

If an entire nest has fallen, the nest can be placed in a wicker basket or kitchen colander and hung in the same tree. The container doesn't matter so long as it's unobtrusive and has excellent drainage. Locating the nest near the original spot increases the probability of success but isn't essential. Often the parents will continue to feed even if the nest is hung in a nearby tree, which may be necessary if the nest accident occurred because a tree fell or was removed.

Parent birds are usually very accepting of the nest being disturbed for a short period of time.

The following are examples of nests being moved entirely that were very successful.

In one case, the nest was removed from a cavity in a building because new siding was being placed on the house. After the siding was installed, we wired a five-gallon bucket on its side under the drain spouting and slid the nest and babies inside. The mother only took a few minutes to return and start feeding the hungry babies.

The second move was an intricately planned project that took some ingenuity. A family owned a farm tractor, and they needed to put it into service. As they were clearing the brush around it, they saw a robin fly out. Upon looking closer, they found a nest under the tractor body containing four blue eggs.

We were called for advice. They wanted to move the tractor, which was needed for their livelihood; but they did say that they could wait for one to two weeks, but no longer than that. There was no chance that the babies would hatch and fledge in that time. There was little chance of a mother robin staying on eggs if the nest had been moved. Also, there was not a nearby location where the nest could be placed.

Because it is the sound of the babies' feeding calls that attracts the parents, waiting for the babies to hatch increased our chances for a successful move of the nest.

During that time, we prepared a new nest site by moving a table next to the tractor, at the same height. The table was situated as close to the nest as possible, and beneath it, we hung an empty wicker basket. This gave the mother time to adjust to the presence of the table. The babies began hatching four days later.

After a few days, when we heard the first babies calling strongly, we moved the entire nest with the babies to the basket beneath the table. The parents began feeding almost immediately. After two more days, the tractor was removed. The farmer resumed his work and so did the robin parents.

That hatch not only thrived and fledged a few weeks later, but the parents chose the same location beneath the table for a second clutch of babies later that season!

CHIMNEY SWIFTS

Chimney swifts are so named because they live in chimneys. The nest is made of twigs and sticky saliva which hardens into a glue-type substance that holds the nest to the wall of a chimney. Occasionally, a single baby bird or the entire nest will fall into the fireplace.

If the babies are feathered and uninjured, they often can be placed back up into the chimney.

Wrap a t-shirt around the brush side of a broom. The swifts will cling to the t-shirt, which is then slowly placed up into the chimney. Lean the broom against the chimney wall with the handle of the broom resting on the damper. The babies will remain on the broom or will cling to the wall of the chimney, thus allowing the mother to continue caring for them.

Remember to remove the broom in the fall prior to the fireplace being used. A chimney cap can be installed before the next spring to prevent chimney swifts from nesting in that chimney again.

KILLDEER

We often hear tales about mother birds pretending to be injured in an effort to lure predators away from the nest. Many birds exhibit this behavior, but the killdeer is the most notable.

Killdeer do not build nests; they choose instead to lay their eggs on a flat, gravel area. Stone driveways are a favored spot for killdeer nests because the spotted eggs blend in perfectly with the gravel.

The first sign of a killdeer nest is not the eggs or a picturesque scene with mother nestled on the eggs, but rather the pitiful sight of a wounded bird barely able to stand on the lawn. These brown birds with horizontal black and white stripes across the face and neck can put on a show that breaks the hardest of hearts.

These are nature's actresses, and performers they are! Attempting to draw attention away from the eggs, they put on a magnificent display, often limping and dragging a wing. An attempt to capture the bird always ends with its miraculous recovery, and the injured bird flies away.

If a killdeer is found "displaying" near your home, carefully inspect the driveway for eggs. If eggs are found, temporarily block off the area, so that cars do not drive over the nest. The eggs hatch in about twenty-five days. Once hatched, the precocial babies can immediately follow the mother, and the nest is abandoned.

Killdeer are exceptional birds in that the parent will raise any baby killdeer. If you find a baby killdeer alone or orphaned, it can be placed near a wild mother, who will adopt it.

BABY BUNNIES

Cottontail babies are the most frequent animal patients in many wildlife rehabilitation centers. In any given year, Red Creek receives over five hundred juvenile cottontails, which equates to one-quarter of our total wildlife patients.

Cottontail nests are often exposed following a gardening accident, mowing the lawn, or when suddenly found by a child or a pet.

The discovery of a cottontail nest does not necessarily constitute an emergency or a need for intervention. If the bunnies were not injured, the nest could be returned to its original condition, and the mother will continue caring for the babies.

Because the success rates of rehabilitating young cottontail rabbits are often much lower than those for other species, every effort must be taken to keep bunnies with the mother when possible.

Two misunderstandings about rabbit nests result in excessive human interference.

The first is the belief that the mother will abandon or kill the babies because the nest was disturbed or the babies were touched. This is a fallacy. The mother will NOT abandon or kill her babies. On rare occasions, she might move them, but she will most likely just continue caring for them as usual.

The second misunderstanding comes from the finder's not seeing the mother after the nest was discovered, convincing her that the nest was actually abandoned. The mother's absence is part of the fundamental biology and defense of the nest. Understanding the behavior of the mother rabbit and why that behavior works to keep the nest from predators is important for the rehabilitator and should be relayed to the finder.

NESTING BEHAVIOR

The location of the nest is essential to its thriving. The spot chosen often has to do with temperature, humidity, and location of first foods for the bunnies nearby; such as dandelion and clover.

The nest remains clean because the baby bunnies cannot defecate or urinate on their own until they are old enough to leave the nest. When the mother visits the nest to feed the babies, she stimulates them and eats the excrement, thereby keeping the nest odor-free.

A nesting bunny's scent glands have not yet developed, and they do not put off an odor of their own. They will remain odorless for much of their juvenile development. They absorb odors around them, becoming odor camouflaged, and blending into the environment.

The mother rabbit does have mature scent glands, however, and leaves a scent wherever she rests. Except for short visits to feed and tend to the kits, she stays away from the nest so that her own odor does not linger.

Although human scent at the nest or on the bunnies will not discourage the mother, it is possible to leave enough human scent at the nest so that a predator might get curious and find the nest. For this reason, handling should be minimized to only that which is necessary.

We are often asked if a nest can be moved because of dangers such as those from dogs. The answer is NO! Because the babies do not put off an odor, even the mother will not be able to find them if they have been moved.

Nesting rabbits consume massive amounts of milk at each feeding. The stomach capacity of young rabbits is two to three times that of most mammal babies; and, therefore, the rabbits require feedings to receive proper nutrition. Newborn bunnies only nurse two to three times in a twenty-four-hour period. Within a week, one-to-two daily feedings are all that is required.

Since the mother's visits are infrequent and brief, her perceived absence results, and a person finding and watching the nest might believe the nest has been abandoned.

TESTING THE NEST

Occasionally an adult rabbit will be found dead near a known nest. The dead adult might or might not be the actual mother. There are two ways that a nest can be tested to determine if the mother is still caring for the babies.

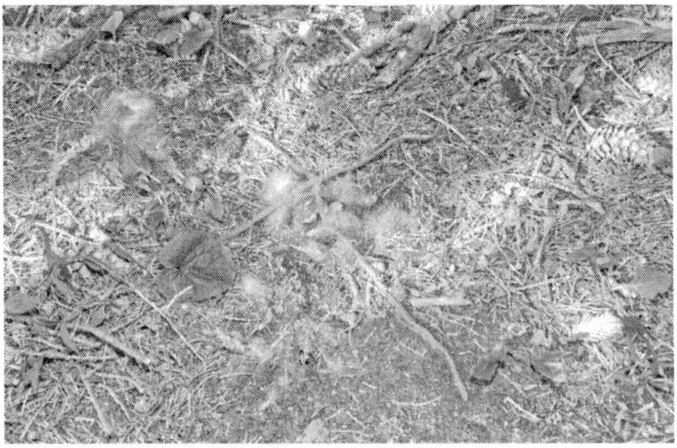

First is the string test. Place two pieces of yarn or string loosely over the nest in the shape of an "X." Because the mother mostly visits at night, this should be done in the early evening. The next morning, check the nest to see if the yarn has been moved. If the nest was untouched, the babies have been orphaned.

Another test is to pick up one or two babies and look at their bellies. In its first week of life, a cottontail's belly skin is very thin and partially transparent. If it's been recently fed, there will be a light-colored triangle in the center of the abdominal area. This is milk in the stomach and indicates that it has been recently fed.

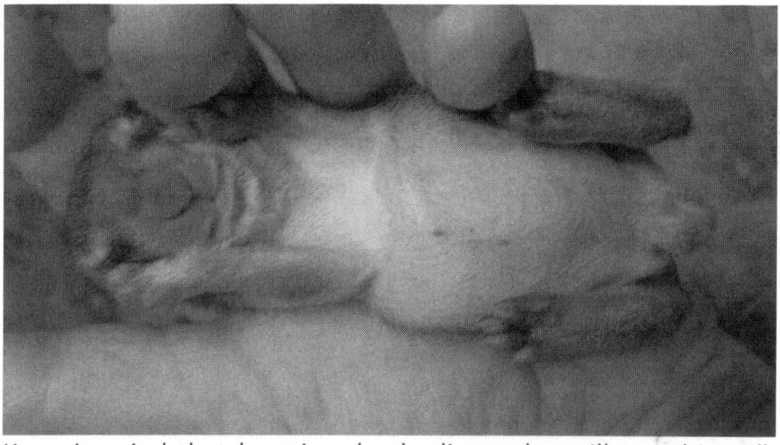

Keep in mind that bunnies slowly digest the milk, so this milk can be observed for up to twelve hours. A recheck twelve to twenty-four hours later will assure you that the mother is still returning and has fed the babies.

IDENTIFYING EMERGENCIES

All visible injuries are an immediate emergency. Gardening accidents, a nest that has been stepped on, and pet attacks often result in injuries. If a single bunny has been injured, perhaps the remaining rabbits can be left in the nest. If the injury to one bunny has left blood in or near the nest, the entire nest is in danger of failing.

A mower accident will often wound or kill one or two babies, while the others are untouched. The blood from the injured bunnies will attract flies, and these flies will lay eggs which will hatch into maggots. This endangers the remaining babies.

Maggots and fly eggs may or may not accompany an open wound. Their presence, however, is a sure sign that the animal is in serious trouble. If left untreated, maggots will burrow into wet tissue or openings in the skin, causing infection and literally eat the animal alive. Most people don't realize that maggots DO NOT need an open wound on an animal's body; they need only constant moisture to develop. Maggots will enter the ears, eyes, mouth, and other orifices.

Any bunny that was in a dog's or cat's mouth should be treated with antibiotics. Dogs, and especially cats, carry bacteria, including *Pasteurella*, in their mouths. *Pasteurella* is highly infectious to wild animals, especially young rabbits. Untreated, the animal can develop a systemic infection that attacks major organs. Once this happens, the animal will die painfully within a few days.

These are quick and easy decisions. As soon as I hear, "My dog or cat had this animal," my immediate response is, "Get it to a wildlife rehabilitator right away!"

There are times when nest disruption requires evacuation of all the bunnies. Flooding any time of year and heavy snowfalls in the spring can be considered a natural disaster for a bunny nest. Construction in an area that removes all the dirt and ground cover may mean that there is no place to rebuild the nest. These are emergencies! Each year, we also receive babies found in soil delivered by truck to a home for landscaping. These are cases where rehabbing the entire nest is a must.

If no emergency exists, every effort must be made to re-nest the bunnies so that the mother can care for them. Cottontails are difficult to rehab; yet in nature, this is a hardy, prolific animal. A carefully re-nested litter of bunnies often flourishes.

INDEPENDENCE

Cottontails are independent when they are five inches long, which usually occurs when they are about 15 to 18 days old. They might remain at or near the nest or wander far. Each individual is different.

This bunny is old enough to care for itself.

At this age, they are still fragile and uncoordinated. They do not run fast and often fall when fleeing danger and so are easily captured by predators. However, their scent glands still have not developed, so they remain odor camouflaged. If they stay still in the right background, they blend in with their surroundings and become visually camouflaged as well.

Blending in is how they survive; and they will continue to be still, even to the point of allowing a person to pick them up. This lack of escape response is often misidentified as a lack of independence, and kidnapping results.

Cottontails of this age can be moved away from areas that are dangerous, such as outside of a fenced dog yard. If moved, they should be placed in a safe area where adequate first foods, such as dandelion and clover, are growing.

Putting a young rabbit under a low-hanging pine tree or in a strong-smelling area will quickly mask any human scent on the baby, thus returning its odor camouflage.

Cottontails, even the juveniles, stress very quickly with handling. When relocating an independent bunny, resist the urge to coddle, pet, and nurture it. These actions can result in the rabbit experiencing cardiogenic shock, a potentially fatal condition, also known as capture myopathy.

To relocate a rabbit, don't carry it in your hands. Instead, place it into a cardboard box and keep the box closed until you are ready to release it. Walk or drive directly to the location. Avoid unnatural sounds such as loud talking and playing the radio.

FAWNS

Each year, Red Creek receives over a hundred calls about foundling fawns. Foundling fawns can be found during a nature hike or seen standing on or near a roadway. Fawns can show up in backyards in rural and urban neighborhoods and have been found lying under carports and on porch steps. They've also been known to stroll into barns, garages, warehouses, and unusual locations where we would never expect to see them.

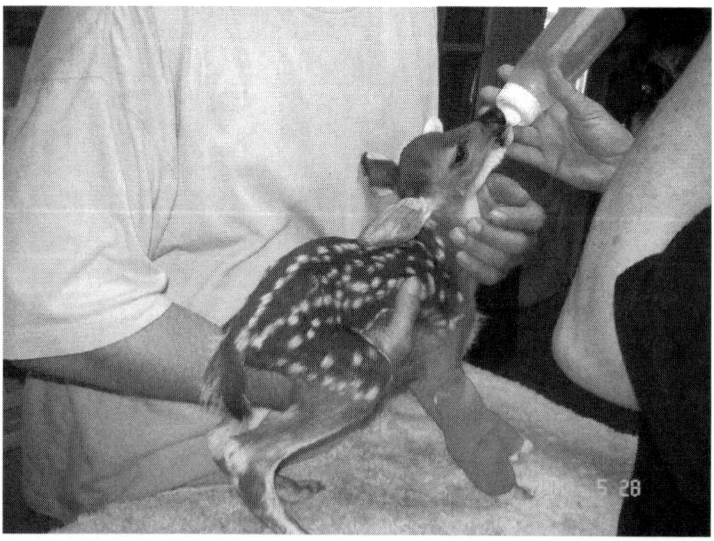

People often find fawns and think that they have been orphaned or abandoned. The fawn will be seen day after day, in the exact same place, alone. They are cute. They appear fragile, and they are hard to resist. It can be difficult to just walk away.

Finding a fawn alone, whether in a natural environment or a completely unnatural setting, does not constitute an emergency. Being alone is part of their early development; and being curious and intelligent animals, they can get bored and wander into the strangest places.

THE DANGER OF INTERFERING

Young fawns lose their fear of humans very easily. Once they feel that people are not a threat, they often seek them out. This attraction can draw them away from the area the mother visits thus causing separation. If someone visits a fawn regularly, it may begin to follow other people who enter the area. This behavior can be interpreted as a fawn having been abandoned or orphaned and results in its being kidnapped by a well-meaning person.

If humanized fawns survive, they will grow very quickly and will soon become adult deer large enough to injure or kill a person. Fawns that have lost their fear of people will carry that lack of fear into adulthood. Although appearing tame, they remain wild animals whose actions and reactions can be unpredictable. Humanized deer can be a real danger to any person they encounter, even to the person who tamed them.

Each year, news stories arise about deer that are kept as pets or raised and released back into the wild that subsequently maul people. Sometimes, those people are family members, friends, neighbors, or complete strangers that the deer encounters. Often these encounters result in a person being injured. Occasionally, a person dies. Almost always, the deer is killed by authorities all because someone tamed it when it was young.

MISUNDERSTANDINGS THAT CAUSE KIDNAPPING

Two misunderstandings about fawns result in excessive interference:

First is the belief that the mother will abandon or kill the fawn because it was touched. This is a fallacy. The mother will NOT abandon her fawn because she smells you on her fawn. Human scent on the fawn can, however, reveal the fawn's location to a predator, such as a fox; therefore, touching should be avoided unless absolutely necessary.

The second misunderstanding comes from the finder's not seeing the mother after the fawn was discovered, which suggests that the baby was abandoned.

The mother's absence is part of the fundamental biology and defense of the young deer. A fawn's scent glands develop as it matures, so a young fawn will have no body odor. This, along with visual camouflage, protects it from predators. The mother doesn't want to place her odor in the area, so she only visits for short periods, often during the night. Her presence endangers her baby, so she must leave it alone.

A fawn can be seen alone in the same area for days or weeks at a time with no evidence of the mother. The fawn's continued health is the only indicator that it's receiving care from its mother.

RESULTS OF FEEDING

Another temptation at "helping" the fawn is often just as deadly: feeding the fawn.

It seems to be human nature to want to feed baby animals. Wildlife rehabilitators are constantly advising the public not to feed baby animals. Suddenly feeding any wild animal, whether that animal is in distress or not, will almost always cause it harm. With fawns, that statement is critical.

If a fawn is truly in trouble, perhaps injured and dehydrated, feeding milk to the baby deer can cause refeeding syndrome, a metabolic disturbance disrupting the amounts of insulin and electrolytes in the bloodstream.

The effects are not immediate. Animals may rally from the sugars and fluid and appear as if they are recovering. Death can occur in three to five days.

This syndrome is almost impossible to reverse. Most animals will die. A wildlife rehabilitator will attempt to give injectable fluids and vitamins, which are also depleted in starvation, but the damage is usually not reversible.

We are often asked by people who find fawns if they should assist a foundling by feeding it, even though it appears healthy. But introducing a new milk formulation will result in the fawn's getting diarrhea, which will attract flies that will lay eggs on the soiled fur around the fawn's tail. Within one day, these eggs will hatch; and the maggots will enter the digestive system making the fawn sick, eventually killing the young deer.

ASSISTING A FAWN IN A DANGEROUS LOCATION

Sometimes fawns will get themselves into a dangerous place, such as on a road or next to a busy roadway. These fawns can be moved away from the road.

Fawns old enough to run can be encouraged to run away from the road until they reach a safer area. Tiny fawns can be carried a hundred yards or so away from the roadway and encouraged to lie down and stay. Don't worry about the mother finding it. When she returns, the fawn will respond to her call.

Be aware that approaching a fawn can be dangerous. A fawn could run out onto the roadway and cause an accident. A larger fawn can kick and injure the person attempting to move it. There is also the danger of the mother doe attacking the person who approached the fawn. Moving a fawn should only be attempted when it can be done safely and by someone who understands the risks.

SIGNS THAT A FAWN IS IN TROUBLE

Fawns found with their dead mother or those born as a result of a pregnant doe being hit by a vehicle, are the only fawns we label as true orphans. These need immediate rescue so that they do not develop problems.

A fawn found in the area where a doe was hit may not necessarily be the fawn of that doe and should not be rescued unless it develops signs of distress.

An orphaned fawn will quickly develop signs of distress indicating that it's in trouble. Dehydration will be visible within a day or so and is indicated by curling of the ears, ruffling of the fur, and dulling of the eyes. Ear-curling is the first sign seen as the rounded edges of the ears will dry and begin to roll back at the tips.

Injuries are often obvious. Punctures from animal attacks and fractured limbs will become infected quickly with maggots and bacteria. Prompt treatment by a wildlife rehabilitator or veterinarian is necessary.

Diarrhea is another life-threatening condition for a fawn. Soiled fur will attract flies and cause maggots to form around the tail as well as the face, between the hooves, and in the developing scent glands on the legs. The maggots will enter the body cavities and begin eating the deer alive. Maggots and maggot eggs are an immediate sign of distress, and action needs to be taken quickly if the fawn is to have a chance of surviving!

Fawns will often be seen lying curled up or on their abdomens, flattening themselves to the ground. However, a fawn lying flat out on its side with its legs extended is in severe distress.

A hungry fawn will cry out for its mother. This is normal. Extreme and continuous vocalizations for an extended period of time can be a sign that the mother is not returning.

Great care must be taken, however, with a crying fawn. The mother may not respond because you are in the area, making you believe that the fawn has been abandoned; and some fawns can be very vocal and demanding naturally. When dealing with a crying fawn, an examination should be done to determine if there are other signs of problems, such as dehydration.

FINDING HELP

Only orphaned, injured, and sick fawns should be assisted. These fawns should be immediately transported to a local wildlife rehabilitator that is permitted to take fawns.

Calling the wildlife rehabilitator first will not only alert them to your emergency but will also enable them to inform you about local laws and regulations. Not all states allow the rehabilitation of deer of any age, including fawns.

Even states that allow rehab may not have a rehabilitator locally or may not allow deer to be rehabbed from certain areas. For example: as of this writing, Pennsylvania allows the rehabilitation of fawns in much of the state, except for quarantine locations where chronic wasting disease is present. The potential for moving the disease to other areas is too great to allow deer to be transported from these areas.

Examining a fawn for signs of a problem.

OPOSSUMS

It's normal for most animal babies to be found for periods of time without mom, but opossums are one of the few babies that are NEVER found alone. They cannot survive on their own.

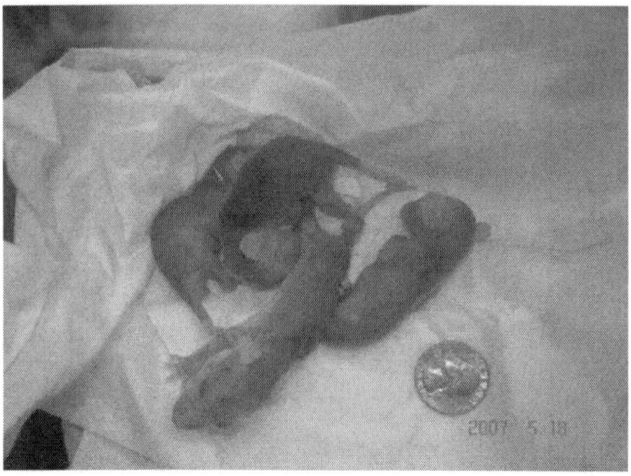

When they are born, opossums are embryonic and only the size of a pencil's eraser. They crawl into the mother's pouch and remain there for about two months. After leaving the pouch, they hitch a ride on mother's back and stay with her until they are six or more inches long excluding their tails.

Mother opossums often are killed on the road; but the babies remain alive, sometimes uninjured, in the pouch or scattered about on the roadway. Check the pouch in mom's abdomen for remaining babies. She can have had up to thirteen.

Sometimes the baby simply falls off the mother. She may keep going, unknowingly abandoning it.

These are true emergencies, because without its mother, a baby opossum will die.

When hungry, an opossum will make a repeated sneezing-type sound. It does not have a cold, it is hungry.

CATCHING BABY OPOSSUMS

If a mother opossum has been killed and the babies have scattered into the surrounding area, you may have to trap the babies.

Take a five-gallon bucket (for small opossums) or a garbage can (for larger ones) and place it against a fence, tree, or other easy-to-climb surface. Place a strong-smelling, opened can of cat food inside the container. The opossums will be able to climb up and jump into the container but will not be able to climb back out.

By leaving the container out all night, and you should catch all the babies in the area.

SQUIRRELS

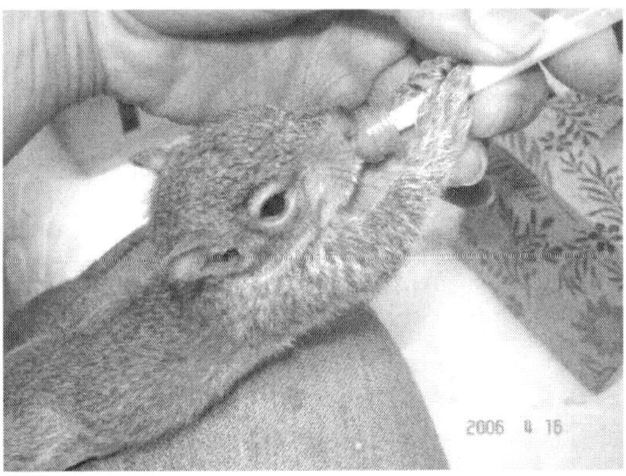

Squirrel nests are often destroyed when a tree is cut down. This may or may not be an emergency. Given the opportunity, the mother will sometimes retrieve an uninjured baby and carry it to a new location, but she will not approach if people are near.

An uninjured baby squirrel can be placed in a box near the tree and watched for a short time from a distance, preferably through a window from indoors. This may result in the mother's rescuing it. Wait a few hours or until dark, but do not leave the babies out past sunset.

Squirrels are one of the only baby animals that typically will "ask for help" when in trouble. A hungry baby squirrel may approach you, often climbing onto your shoes or climbing up your pant leg.

How can you tell if a young squirrel is old enough to be on its own? Look at the hairs on the tail. If they stand upright, fanning out completely perpendicular to the tail, it is weaned.

SIGNS OF A PROBLEM

Injury such as broken limbs

Bleeding, bruising, and "crustiness" around the nostrils (a sign of a concussion needing medical treatment)

Screaming babies on the ground or clinging to trees

Maggots or fly eggs on the fur or in the ears

CAPTURE

If you have a situation in front of you and are looking for quick instructions, please take the time to review the previous section. The choices you make and the actions you take will not only affect the animal you are rescuing, but they can also affect your life and health as well as that of your family and pets.

You have a wildlife situation! You are aware of the dangers to yourself and the stress that capture will place on the animal. You have also determined that the animal needs help. So how do you safely capture a wild animal?

Each species is different, and each situation has its own problems. Some animals are easily captured with nets and blankets while others require the use of gloves. It takes experience to perfect these techniques; and even with experience and expertise, you can be injured. No book or written instructions can teach these methods safely, but we do have one way that works for most situations.

THE BOX-OVER METHOD

The best way to protect yourself is to never touch the animal in the first place. When giving directions for wildlife capture, my preferred instruction is the "box-over method." With this method, you can capture most animals safely without touching the animal, and the animal never touches you.

To capture an animal with this method, you need an appropriately sized container, such as a cardboard box, that is large enough in which to fit the animal snugly. The box needs to be strong enough to keep the animal from escaping, breaking out, or (for mammals such as woodchucks) chewing through. For large animals that are too strong for a cardboard box, a metal trash can works well.

This capture container will also be your transport device and will therefore need ventilation. Most cardboard boxes breathe without additional ventilation, but if you are planning on using a container that will be airtight, several small holes placed near the top of the container will allow for air exchange.

When capturing the animal, this container will be slipped over the animal, upside-down, thereby trapping the animal in the container against the ground.

You also will need a stiff, thin piece of cardboard, metal, plastic, or wood that is larger than the opening of the container. You can use the lid of the box if there is one. Once the container is over the animal, slide this stiff sheet or lid under the container between the animal and the ground. You will also need tape to secure the two pieces together. Duct tape or a strong packing tape both work well for this.

Once you have everything you will need, approach the animal slowly. If the animal is mobile, you may need several people to cut off its escape routes. Make sure the direction away from you does not have hazards such as traffic, water, or thick briars to where the animal may flee and experience further injury.

When you are close enough, quickly place the container over the animal trapping it against the ground. Hold the container down firmly for a moment until the animal stops struggling.

Slowly work the thin, stiff board under the edge of the container and slide it between the animal and the ground. You may have to use a gentle sawing motion to get the board completely underneath or wiggle the container to push the animal on top of the board. Work slowly until the board is past all the edges of the container.

Once done, you have successfully contained the animal without touching it. You can now secure the lid or stiff sheet to the container with heavy tape. Very carefully roll the container until it is upright and secure the "packaging" some more.

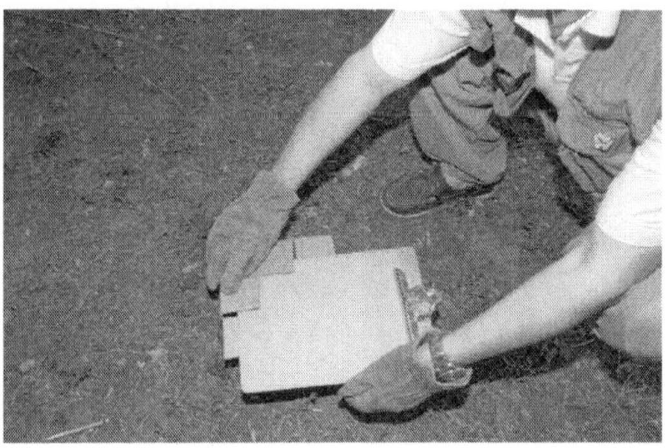

HOW TO CAPTURE A DUCK

Ducks pose unique problems when injured. If they can't fly, they can still run and swim; and, even injured, will take to water for protection. Attempts to capture injured waterfowl often result in the proverbial "wild goose chase" and often end in failure. It can be done, however, with the proper planning, techniques, and equipment.

More than one person is usually needed to catch waterfowl. If the bird is on land and can be lured in with food, two people will usually suffice. If the bird is on water or must be chased onto land, many more hands will be needed.

HAND CAPTURE

Many people think nets are the easiest way to catch ducks, but in my experience, even the tamest hand-fed ducks will flee at the sight of a net. Anything out of the ordinary will send them scurrying away from you.

If the duck is accustomed to being hand-fed, you can lure it in with seed or bread. Sit on the ground and try to coax the bird to come close to you. Patience is the key to gaining its trust. You will only have one chance, so make it a good one. Once the bird knows you are trying to catch it, it will not come near you again.

When the bird has come close enough, you can throw a towel or sheet over it. If the bird is nervous, even the strangeness of a cloth will be enough to scare it away. In that case, you may have to grab the bird with your hands.

Don't grab the neck, wings, or legs as this could injure the bird further.

To grab a duck successfully on land, position your hands over the top of its wings and gently push the bird toward the ground. Once you have the bird and wings controlled, have a second person approach and drape a towel or sheet over the bird's head.

Lift the bird gently, holding its wings securely against its body, and place the bird inside a cardboard box that has fold-in flaps. While you are securely holding the bird in the bottom of the box, have a second person fold the flaps in. Do not let go until the last flap is being folded closed. Hold the flaps in place while the other person secures the box with tape.

LAND CAPTURE

A wary duck or goose that is mobile on land will need to be corralled into a trap or safe area for hand-capture. Several people will be needed to cut off the bird's escape routes and encourage the bird to flee into your trap.

A careful examination of the area will offer suggestions on which way to chase the bird. You want to avoid chasing the bird into the water or areas that may be dangerous.

An empty garage, barn, or fenced yard can serve as a corral area, as can several people with nets or blankets hiding in a small area.

Your chase group would then create a semicircle around the bird with the opening toward the planned capture area.

To extend your semicircle with fewer people, you can cover a larger area by holding blankets between each person, creating a visible "wall" that the bird believes it cannot pass. One person can create the same effect with two blankets and two long sticks (such as broom handles) held out to the side as shown in the photos below.

Do not run after the bird. It may take some time and patience to get the bird tired enough so that it stops running. You want to tire the bird while conserving your energy so the bird tires before you do.

WATER CAPTURE

WARNING

When working near water, beware of soft ground and mud. You could sink and be stranded, thus requiring rescue yourself.

Always work in teams when rescuing in a wetlands area.

The trick to capturing a bird that's on the water is to get it to flee to the land where it can be captured using the techniques outlined previously. How the bird is persuaded to leave the water will depend on the size of the lake or pond involved.

If the pond is small enough to cast a fishing line across it, chasing the bird from the water can be quite easy.

Have two people stand on either side of the pond. On one side, group #1 has a casting pole for fishing with a heavy weight to cast completely across the pond. On the other side, group #2 has two long pieces of floating rope or plastic carpenter's tape (orange works best), each long enough to reach across the pond.

Group #1 casts the fishing line across the pond to group #2. The end of each rope or tape is loosely tied to the end of the fishing line; and group #1 then reels the line back in, bringing the rope ends toward it. After removing the fishing line, each person takes an end of one rope and moves apart, stretching the rope over the pond in an "X" fashion. Keep each rope taut about 18 inches above the water.

Working together, you can now approach the duck, encouraging it to move with the rope. If the duck attempts to jump the rope, raise the rope and slap it off the water. If the bird dives under the water, wait for it to surface and start over.

Many ducks will leave the water right away, but others may continuously avoid the rope by diving under it or jumping over it. Again, patience is the key, and you will have to tire the duck until it leaves the water.

Loon Rescue

When the body of water is extremely large, it will be necessary for you to use motorboats or remote-controlled toy boats to chase the bird toward the landing you wish it to take. Two or more manned motorboats can string the same type of orange carpenter's tape or floating rope between the boats to encourage the bird to move toward land. Once the bird is on land, have a team waiting to begin the land chase toward a trap.

GEESE

With a few modifications, an injured goose can be captured in the same manner as a duck. Because of their size, geese can be dangerous and can injure you if they are handled incorrectly. They cannot be hand-captured in the same manner as a duck.

Geese have a hidden weapon that is quite formidable. This weapon, called the *alula,* is a sharp bone protruding from the wrist area of the wing. With a strong slap of the wing, the *alula* can cut skin and cause bruises and contusions. A well-directed blow to the head can stun a person or cause a mild concussion.

These birds are best hand-captured by having two people throw and hold a blanket down over the bird. A box can then be worked over the bird, and capture is completed by using the box-over method outlined on page 68.

HERONS, EGRETS, AND OTHER FISHING BIRDS

Fishing birds with long pointed beaks are among the most dangerous birds to handle. They have adapted to prey on fish and have deadly aim with their beaks. Because many have long necks and legs, they can extend their reach much farther than one would expect. When you are approaching a fishing bird, it is quite possible that the bird can reach out and injure you before you are even close enough to touch it.

Great Blue Heron

We never work with these types of birds without eye protection that covers the eyes completely, including the sides. Eyeglasses do not offer enough protection because the slightest mishap can cause severe eye damage and even permanent blindness. This is not a bird with which to take chances; for if you do, it may cost you your sight!

Note the eye protection on both handlers

Wearing both eye protection and gloves, use the box-over method outlined on page 68. Approach the bird from its front and keep the box between you and the bird. Once you are close enough, place the box down over the bird to enclose it.

If you cannot effectively capture the bird in this manner, you may need to use a blanket to first render it helpless. You may also need two people for this method; and again, both persons must wear eye protection and gloves.

Walk toward the bird with the blanket in front of you and drape it over the bird completely. Once the bird is covered, feel through the blanket for the beak. Hold the beak securely while a second person lifts the body of the bird. DO NOT LET GO OF THAT BEAK!

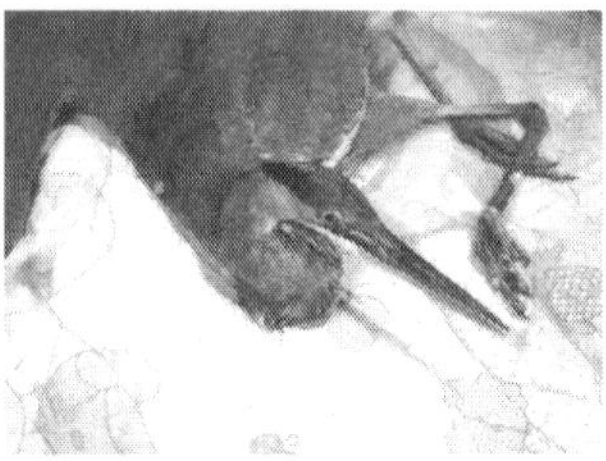

Even incapacitated, this bird is capable of inflicting severe injury

Working together, lower the bird and the blanket into the travel container. Place the lid on the container or fold in the flaps of the box while still holding on to that beak. Release the beak as the box is quickly closed and secured.

LOONS AND GREBES

Loons and grebes are also fishing birds with long necks and sharp beaks. The same precautions about eye protection need to be followed as with herons and egrets.

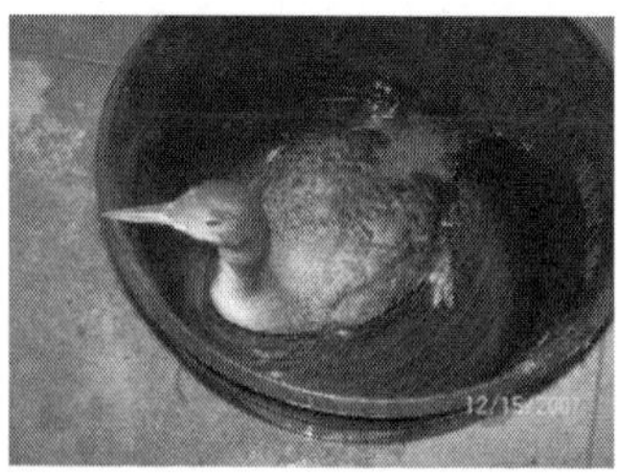

Arctic Loon

There is one exception that is significant, and although it aids in an easy capture, it is the very reason that the birds often become incapacitated; loons and grebes cannot walk.

The legs on a loon-type bird are adapted for swimming and hunting fish underwater (very much like a penguin or seal). The legs are short and set far back and to the sides. The body and chest are quite heavy, which makes it impossible for the bird to stand up on its legs.

Loon Release. Again, notice the eye protection.

Loons and grebes live exclusively on large bodies of water, leaving only to nest by crawling up on the bank, a sand bar, or a large snag. To fly, they must first gain speed by swimming below the surface, then breaking above the surface, and flapping their wings while running on top of the water. The body of water must be sufficiently large to allow the bird to gain enough momentum before reaching land.

While in flight, these birds look for large bodies of water on which to land. Occasionally, a wet roadway or parking lot can be mistaken for water, and the bird will crash on the hard surface and become stranded. This often happens in winter when snow-and-ice-covered roads are mistaken for partially frozen lakes and rivers. Once on the ground, the bird can neither walk nor fly. If it is not rescued, it will become injured from resting on the hard surface or it will die.

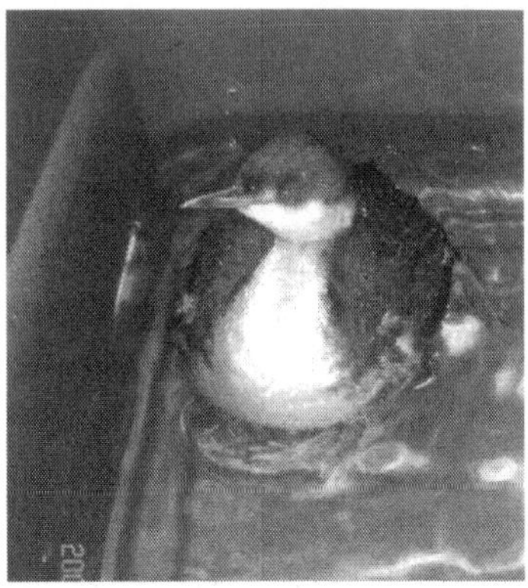

Horned Grebe

In this case, the bird is usually not injured except for small cuts and scrapes on its feet. Often, the bird only needs to be returned to a large, open body of water where it can resume its normal life.

Do not mistake this bird's inability to move for helplessness! These birds have the same long neck and pointed beak as a heron with just as accurate an aim. This bird will immediately strike for the eyes, and anyone attempting a rescue needs to wear full eye protection.

RAPTORS

Raptors offer an additional challenge to capture because they use both their feet and beaks for protection. The beaks are curved and sharp, designed for tearing flesh. A bite from a raptor can inflict a serious wound, although the feet and talons are its primary weapons. The talons of a great horned owl are about an inch long, and the estimated power of their grip is from 500 to 1,500 pounds per square inch. Even a small raptor, such as an American kestrel or a screech owl, can inflict an open, painful wound; what the smaller raptors lack in size, they seem to make up for with tenacity.

Because of their foot strength, no attempt for capture should ever be made without gloves and eye protection! All-leather welding gloves will protect your hands from most raptors except the larger birds such as great horned owls.

This red-tailed hawk nestling (above)and the juvenile great horned owl (below) already have large, powerful feet.

Although they can fight fiercely even when injured, raptors must be handled carefully to prevent further injury. Every precaution must be taken to avoid feather damage through handling, since feathers must be in top condition for raptors to survive once released. The box-over method (described on page 68) is your best choice for capture.

Covering a daytime raptor with a blanket will quiet it quickly. Hawks especially become calm in the dark. This can prevent escape while minimizing further damage, giving you a chance to get a better grip on the bird.

A severely injured raptor, or one that is in shock, may lie face down, allowing you to pick it up. With the bird face-down and its head away from you, place your hands about half way down the back on each side of the bird to control its wings. Slide your fingers down under the bird until you feel its legs, keeping your thumbs above to hold the wings. Pull the legs back toward the tail, grasping the body, wings, tail, and legs in one grip. Picking the bird up in this manner also allows you to place the bird feet down and facing away from you in the holding box.

Often the bird will try to flee or fight you. After attempting to flee and failing or after being cornered, a raptor will turn and face you. It may puff out its feathers, making itself appear large and fierce in an attempt to scare you away. It may vocalize, click its beak, or make other gestures to back you down. It will then roll back on its tail, aiming its exposed feet (its primary weapons) at you.

Defensive posture of birds of prey

Remember, no matter how fierce the bird is acting, it is extremely frightened and fighting for its life. The capture method you choose should minimize its fear.

If you cannot use a blanket or box because of the terrain or location, then you will need to grab the bird. One method is to allow the bird to grab your gloved hand, and then you grab its legs from behind, between the fingers of your other hand. Getting one finger between its legs will help keep the bird from twisting. If the bird releases its hold on you, you can then support its chest with your free hand.

This last method does have many drawbacks and should only be used as a last resort. You cannot grab a bird in this manner if there is a possibility of a leg or hip injury. Holding a bird this way also does not control its wings, which will flap frantically, probably in your face (another good reason to be wearing your goggles).

OTHER SUGGESTIONS

The box-over method may not be necessary in all situations. We offer the following suggestions with the additional warning for you to use common sense and to think **"Safety First."**

Never put a bird in a wire cage. Wire cages (even bird and parrot cages) will fray and break feathers, which the bird needs to fly perfectly. Damaged feathers will impede its ability to survive and may result in an unnecessarily extended rehabilitation time.

Choose a container that is large enough so as not to damage feathers, yet small enough to prevent excessive movement.

Wild animals will feel more secure if they cannot see outside the container. This is easily achieved if using a box or storage tub. If you are using a plastic airline crate, it must be covered with a blanket to obstruct the animal's view.

Keep baby animals together to share body heat. One inventive way to transport baby opossums or squirrels is to place them together inside a pillow case. Tie the pillowcase shut and place it inside the transport box.

Never lay an unconscious animal on its back. Lay an unconscious bird or mammal face-down, slightly to the side.

Give a bird something to hold on to. Place a baby blanket, sweatshirt, or t-shirt in the bottom of the container for the bird to grasp with its feet. Never place bath towels or bed sheets inside the container with the animal, as these can unravel and create an entanglement.

Attempt to pad the animal. Fill the container over half full with finely shredded newspaper. This will support the animal on all sides, keeping it from rolling or banging against the inside of the container. Blankets padding the sides of the box will serve the same purpose. Again, make sure the cloth cannot unravel and ensnare the animal.

When packaging a mammal for transport, use the same considerations you would use for a bird. Make sure the animal cannot see outside the container and that it has proper ventilation. Supply padding such as shredded newspaper or blankets.

The biggest danger with transporting a mammal is escape. Many mammals can chew their way out of a cardboard box or plastic crate in just a few minutes. Make sure the container you're using is secure enough to confine the animal.

POST CAPTURE - WHAT NOW?

Once an animal is captured, the best possible outcome would be its immediate transport to a wildlife veterinarian or rehabilitator. If you have prepared in advance and have the phone number with you, contacting them would be your next step.

Be prepared to transport the animal yourself. Most rehabilitators work on a volunteer basis with very limited funds. Many do not have the resources to pick up animals and need your assistance to get that animal into the rehabilitation system.

If you do not have the contact information handy or if there is no immediate answer, you may have to hold the animal for a short time.

TRANSPORTATION

At some point, you will have to transport the animal either to the rehabilitator or to your home for temporary holding. This sounds easy, and with a little common sense, it is. How the animal is transported will have a great effect on its stress level. The following guidelines will help reduce the animal's anxiety during the ride.

- Be safe traveling. Don't allow excitement and adrenaline to take over. Follow the speed limits and obey all the traffic laws. You can't help the animal if you are injured in an accident.
- Keep the animal in the dark and remove any visual stimulation. If the animal is in a cardboard box, this has already been accomplished. If the animal can see out,

cover the container completely with a towel, blanket, or coat.

- The best place to position the box for transport is on the floor behind the front passenger's or driver's seat. If this is not possible, place the box as centrally located in the vehicle as possible. This will lessen movement when turning and driving over rough roadways. Secure the container with a seatbelt or by tying it down to prevent rolling.
- DO NOT transport animals in the trunk of a car or in the open bed of a pickup truck.
- DO NOT play the radio. Music may be soothing to you, but it is completely foreign to a wild animal. Dark and quiet are the keys to a stress-free trip.
- DO NOT smoke. Just as the radio may be a stress factor, the smell of smoke can heighten an animal's feeling of danger.
- Think of all possible causes of stress and try to eliminate them during the ride.
- Avoid the temptation to peek. Animals often calm down and become quiet during transport; and you may fear that the animal has gotten worse or has expired. A slight opening of the container may be all the animal needs to encourage an escape attempt, and you do not want the animal loose in your car.

TEMPORARY HOLDING

It may be necessary to house the animal temporarily until contact with a rehabilitator can be made. This is a critical time during the rescue where people make the worst mistakes trying to help the animal. It is during this time that people often try to feed the animal, examine it, and begin critical care. These actions often result in a worsening of the animal's condition, a complication of its situation, or even its death.

What the animal needs during this time is
WARMTH – DARKNESS – QUIET!

Again, avoiding the temptation to peek, place the box in an unused spare bedroom or bathroom and close the door. Keep everyone, especially children and pets, away from the animal.

If the animal is very young, you may need to supply supplemental heat to keep it warm. Placing a heating pad set on LOW under half of the container will allow the animal to move toward or away from the heat to regulate its own body temperature. If a heating pad is not available, a hot water bottle or soda bottle filled with warm water and placed inside a sock can be a comfortable heat source for the animal to snuggle against.

PET OWNERS - BEWARE

If you have pets in your home, be aware that they can contract many diseases and parasites common in wildlife. This is especially true if you own pet birds. You do not want your attempt at rescuing a wild animal to result in the loss of a beloved pet.

If you have pets in your home, you may not wish to bring a wild animal inside at all. Housing it temporarily on an outside porch or in a garage may be a safer choice to protect your pets.

To ensure that cross-contamination does not occur, it is advisable to shower and change clothing before handling any susceptible pets and discard anything that came into contact with the wild animal.

TEMPORARY CARE

WHY SHOULD WE NOT FEED ANIMALS?

It is a basic human instinct to feed an animal to comfort it, especially when it comes to baby animals. However, food is the last thing most animals need when in distress. In the case of an injured animal or one suffering from dehydration, food can kill that animal!

An animal that has suffered injury, exposure, and lack of food for any length of time will also be suffering from dehydration. If the animal is dehydrated, fluids must be stabilized first or it will not be able to process food at all. If the animal eats, the food often lies in the stomach or crop and decomposes without being digested, which complicates its condition.

Many animals are also in a catabolic state, which means the body is drawing energy from its tissues, fat, and even its muscles. When a starved animal is suddenly fed carbohydrates, such as when a baby animal is fed milk, "refeeding syndrome" may occur.

When such an animal is suddenly given food, the body attempts to shift back to utilizing food, which can result in fluid and electrolyte imbalances and vitamin deficiencies. Insulin is released, causing salts and electrolytes to move from the blood to the body tissues, leaving dangerously low blood levels.

Although life-threatening, the effects are not immediate. The animal might rally from the sugars and fluid and appear okay, but the body's systems begin to fail in three to five days.

Refeeding syndrome is almost impossible to reverse. Most animals will die. A rehabilitator can attempt to give injectable fluids and vitamins, but the damage is usually done.

Wildlife rehabilitators avoid refeeding syndrome by following strict rehydration regimens of injectable fluids prior to the introduction of any food products. Success, however, is dependent upon the person who originally found the animal being able to resist the overwhelming urge to feed it before taking it to the rehabilitator.

The same is done in human medicine. If you were in a car accident, had suffered cuts, bruises, and fractures, and an ambulance crew came to your aid, *they would not feed you.*

Once you reached the hospital, you would be examined, medicated, and have received I.V. fluids, but *you would not be fed.*

If you needed surgery, you might receive more fluids, possibly blood, and more medication; and when you woke up, *you would not be fed.*

Just like a human trauma case, an injured animal needs first to be stabilized and rehydrated. Food is then gradually introduced often initially in the form of a liquid diet. Rushing this important step can be just enough to push a compromised animal over the edge.

EXCEPTIONS TO THE "DO NOT FEED" RULE

Of course, for every rule there is an exception. With animals, that exception is *very tiny birds.*

HUMMINGBIRDS

Hummingbirds have an extremely high metabolism, and if their feeding intervals are interrupted or extended, they can shut down rather quickly. Hummingbirds need to eat every fifteen to thirty minutes during daylight hours. Even when they are injured, they still need to eat continuously.

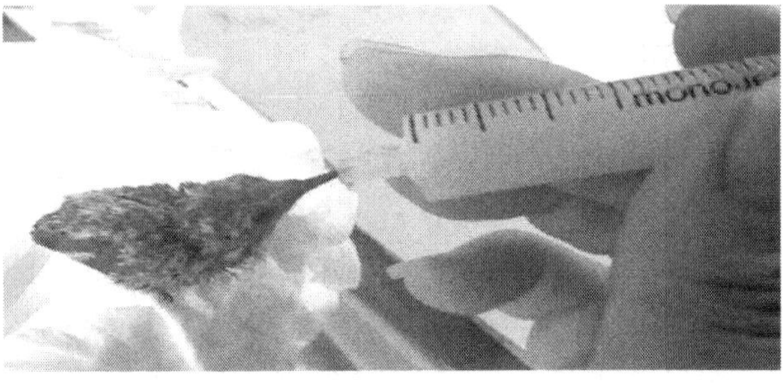

Hummingbirds can be offered a drink by dipping their beak into a hummingbird feeder, or they can be fed from a dropper. Offer nectar or sugar water (one-quarter cup of sugar dissolved in one cup of water) every fifteen to twenty minutes.

If using a dropper, do not squeeze out the nectar. Placing the very tip of the beak in the nectar should be enough to encourage the bird to drink on its own. It is a wondrous thing to watch a hummingbird drink, as its tongue will quickly flick in and out as the nectar volume decreases. If the hummingbird can perch or remain upright on its own, making the nectar available at all times will keep the bird hydrated and stable until transport can be arranged.

BABY SONGBIRDS

Tiny baby birds, such as sparrows and finches, also cannot survive long without hydration and calories. Hand-feeding these baby birds can be quite dangerous to them, since too much food or the wrong liquidity can result in aspiration.

Baby birds must be supported and kept in a tight, nest-like container. This can be achieved by placing tissues in an appropriately-sized berry box, margarine container, or small bowl. If baby birds are kept on a flat or slippery surface, their legs may spread, causing injury or deformity.

If you need to keep a baby bird for a few hours, first make sure the bird is warm and active before attempting to introduce anything by mouth. Stabilize the bird's body temperature by placing half the box on a heating pad set on low. If the nestling is still chilled, drop a tissue on top of the bird to help maintain its warmth.

The first offerings should be small drops of liquid to increase hydration. Pedialyte or Gatorade mixed half-and-half with water will do. If these are unavailable, you can boil plain, non-diet cola to remove the carbonation and then mix half-and-half with water.

Tiny portions given every few minutes will increase hydration while reducing the chances of aspiration or drowning. A small, hobby paintbrush is a simple tool that works quite well for delivering a single drop of liquid at a time.

Most baby birds can be encouraged to open their beaks for you. Sometimes tapping lightly on the container (simulating a mother landing on the nest) will trigger a feeding response. With the baby's mouth open (called "gaping"), place one drop at a time as far back into the mouth as possible.

If the baby will not gape, DO NOT force-feed the bird; some birds, such as doves, do not eat in this manner.

If the baby bird needs to be kept for longer than a few hours, you may need to begin feeding the bird. For almost all songbird species, dry kitten food is an excellent temporary replacement. Soak the dry kitten food in water until soft and then mix to a pudding-like texture.

Dab a small paintbrush in the mixture and place it at the back of the bird's throat behind the glottis or airway (see picture below).

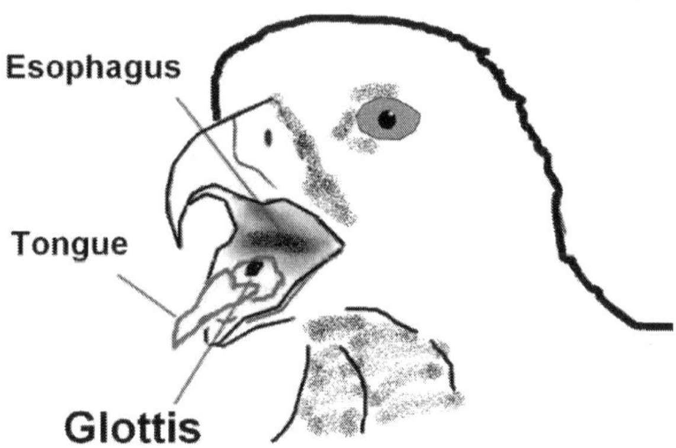

Using the paintbrush, pick up small amounts of the kitten food and place it far back into the gaping mouth. Wait for the bird to swallow before offering more food. Small amounts fed every fifteen minutes will increase the bird's strength and supply the energy it needs until transport can be arranged.

Please be aware that these directions are for TEMPORARY EMERGENCY CARE ONLY!

These actions do not supply the necessary nutrition for proper growth and development and are only intended to keep a small bird alive until transport to a licensed rehabilitator can be arranged.

CLEAN UP

Once the emergency is over, and the animal is back in the environment or with a rehabilitator, be sure to clean and disinfect everything with which the animal came into contact. This is especially important if you have pets or small children.

If you used a cardboard box for capture and transport, it should be discarded or burned. Any bedding you used should also be discarded.

If you used a pet carrier or another container you wish to keep, all urine, blood, and fecal matter should first be removed with detergent. Hydrogen peroxide is excellent for removing blood. Rinse thoroughly and be sure all organic matter has been removed, because organic material cannot be properly disinfected.

Once the container is clean, you are ready to disinfect. Dilute one-part chlorine bleach with ten parts of water and thoroughly drench the surface with the solution. Allow it to remain wet for at least ten or more minutes before rinsing. Allow it to dry.

You also should shower and launder your clothing to remove any parasites and other contaminants.

EMERGENCY CARE

I am not recommending performing first aid on any animal, but there are a few life-threatening conditions that, if not immediately corrected, may cause the animal to die before transportation can be accomplished. There are life-threatening conditions such as bleeding, airway obstruction, hypothermia, and hyperthermia, that you may be able to alleviate if you can safely do so. These conditions can be quickly identified with a cursory glance and do not require a close physical examination.

Again, as always, your safety (and that of the animal) is your primary concern. When presented with a life-threatening condition, it is important that you work quickly and efficiently to avoid unnecessary handling and additional stress.

ALLEVIATING LIFE-THREATENING CONDITIONS

As in human medicine, follow the ABCs!

Airway

Breathing

Circulation (heartbeat and severe bleeding)

AIRWAY AND BREATHING

If the animal has an obstructed airway, attempt to remove the obstruction using an adapted Heimlich maneuver. Hold a small animal upright or put a large animal on its side. Apply force/pressure with fingers or fist just below the sternum in an upward motion (toward the head) quickly, five times. Repeat as necessary.

Remove any visible obstructions. Do NOT put your fingers into the mouth of an animal! If the animal is unconscious, and you can see the foreign object in its throat, attempt to remove it with long forceps or a similar instrument. BE CAREFUL to not push the obstruction down farther.

Discharge can be wiped out of the mouth or nostrils with a swab or suctioned with an eyedropper or a turkey baster.

Reposition the head, so the airway is open.

Any "sucking" wounds (punctures that have entered the airway or respiratory system) can be sealed with an airtight bandage made with plastic wrap and gauze taped tightly to the area.

BLEEDING

- Apply direct pressure with a gauze pad to any bleeding wound(s).
- Do not remove the cloth.
- If blood soaks the material, add another layer on top.
- A bandage may be wrapped around the cloth and taped in place.

Blood Feathers are new, growing feathers that still have a blood supply in the vein. If broken or torn, these feathers will bleed profusely. Apply direct pressure by squeezing the feather shaft closed. The bleeding should stop quickly. Do not attempt to pull blood feathers out, as this procedure can be painful and dangerous to the bird and should be left to a professional.

HYPOTHERMIA (LOW BODY TEMPERATURE)

Lack of calories, shock, and exposure can result in low body temperature. Many young animals are not self-regulating and cannot produce their own body heat. Signs of hypothermia include shivering, sluggishness, dull or slow response to stimuli, shallow breathing, and coma. Infant animals may not show all the signs because of an undeveloped reflex response. Supplying supplemental heat will help stabilize the patient before it reaches the rehabilitation center or veterinarian.

Efforts must be made to warm an animal without overheating or burning it. Supplemental heat in the field can be obtained by using instant hand warmers or by filling a soda or water bottle with warm water and placing any of which inside a sock or wrapping it in a t-shirt. Allow the animal to snuggle up to the warmth, leaving it enough room to move away should it become too warm.

If the animal cannot be immediately transported to the rehabilitation center or veterinarian, maintain a source of heat by placing a heating pad under the container. Set the heating pad on LOW and position half of the box over the pad so the animal can move away from the heat source.

HYPERTHERMIA (HEAT STROKE)

The opposite of hypothermia is hyperthermia, or being over heated. Baby animals that have been exposed to the elements are often cold and sluggish. Occasionally, that infant animal will lie helplessly in the sun and actually bake. We have had people find cold animals and place them under heating lamps or on heating pads hoping to warm the animal before calling us, essentially "cooking" the animal. If the animal has been exposed to extreme heat, and the body feels hot, it must be cooled to avoid organ and neurological damage.

Overheated animals should NOT be doused with cold water; instead, cover them with cool, wet towels for transport and/or bathe them in tepid water to help bring the body temperature down. Rubbing alcohol applied to the footpads can also help.

TARS AND GLUE

Many animals are presented to us after having been stuck on flypaper or on a rodent glue-board. Many others come in covered with tar or another sticky substance such as pine sap. Animals can also be found stuck in fresh tar on a roof or driveway.

This type of emergency needs immediate intervention before the animal is even moved. If the animal is left untreated, its struggles will further ensnare it, exposing more of its skin to the substance and possibly blocking its airway. In an effort to clean itself, the animal may ingest some of the product, possibly resulting in poisoning.

Do not attempt to pull the animal loose! Doing so will injure the animal further, not only destroying feathers and fur but also tearing the skin and causing tremendous pain and stress.

Do not use harsh chemicals to try to remove the glue or tar! Instead, coat the substance with a light, safe oil such as cooking oil or mineral oil. This will immediately stop the adhesive effect and protect the animal from further involvement.

If the animal is stuck on glue paper or glue board that can be moved, all you need to do is coat the board or paper with the oil (not the animal) and transport the animal that way. The oil covering on the trap will render the rest of the glue harmless.

If the animal is covered with a sticky substance such as tar, lightly coat the animal itself in the areas involved to keep the animal from sticking to itself and the transport box.

An animal that is caught in the tar on a roof or roadway must be removed before transport. To safely remove the animal, follow these instructions:

- For animals that are capable of biting, scratching, or injuring you once they are free, protect yourself from bites and scratches by wearing heavy leather gloves.

- For other animals, it's best to wear latex or rubber gloves when possible to keep the ensuing mess off your own skin.
- Drench a clean paintbrush, cotton swab, or paper towel with cooking oil or mineral oil and slowly work the oil between the animal and the sticky surface.
- Keep refilling the brush and work slowly to ensure that fur, feathers, and skin are not torn loose. Do not pull. The oil will liquefy the tar, but it does take a little bit of time and patience. WORK SLOWLY!
- As the animal is worked free, be ready to wrap it in a towel or rag to soak up the extra oil.
- Place the animal in a box with paper towels and transport it as soon as possible.

Even if the animal seems fine and is completely free, it should still be taken to a rehabilitation center. The oil needs to be safely removed from the animal, and the animal needs to be observed for a few days for toxic effects from exposure to the adhesive.

MORE INFORMATION

There are many situations that rehabilitators see repeatedly when wildlife is found. The following is offered to help with further study and understanding about wildlife rescue and helping wildlife.

WHAT IS RABIES?

Rabies is a fatal disease caused by a virus that attacks the central nervous system of warm-blooded animals. All mammals can get rabies, including pets, livestock, and humans. The most commonly affected animals are raccoons, skunks, foxes, bats, and domestic cats.

The rabies virus travels slowly via the nervous system until it reaches the brain. In most species, the time from infection to disease is two to twelve weeks, but some animals have been known to carry the virus for up to a year. Once the virus reaches the brain and clinical signs appear, death follows in two weeks or less. This is also when the virus reaches the saliva and can infect others through exposure. In most animals (bats are an exception), the virus is only transmissible during this last stage of the disease. Once this last stage is reached, rabies is ALWAYS fatal.

Rabies is most often contracted through a bite or scratch, but it can also be transmitted when the saliva or brain tissue of an infected animal comes in contact with an open cut or mucous membranes such as the eyes.

Clinical signs in wild animals can vary greatly and should not be used to judge whether an animal is rabid. Some common signs are changes in normal behavior, unnatural friendliness or aggression, foaming at the mouth, blindness, and paralysis. Some animals, however, die with no visible signs.

Extra precautions MUST be taken with animals in your area that are known to carry rabies. If you think you have had a possible exposure, seek medical advice from your doctor immediately or call your state's department of health. They will instruct you on the steps necessary to protect your health and have the animal tested for rabies.

20 WAYS TO HELP WILDLIFE EVERY DAY

1. KEEP CATS AND DOGS INSIDE! Roaming pets are the number-one cause of injury to baby wildlife.
2. Do not feed wildlife. Attracting large numbers of animals to any given area can hasten the spread of diseases, including rabies. (See 19.)
3. Teach your children to respect wildlife and emphasize a "Hands-Off" policy. This includes nests and eggs.
4. Adjust mower blades to their highest level. Walk the area to be mowed and check for rabbit nests (these are very difficult to spot). If you do know of a nest, mark it and mow around it. In less than two weeks, the nest will be empty.

5. Do birds fly into your windows? Hang a silhouette of a hawk in the window, place vertical pinstripes on the window, or leave the windows "dirty" to reduce reflection.
6. Place bird feeders away from shrubs where cats can hide.
7. Dispose of garbage properly and cut all six-pack rings so wildlife cannot get entangled.
8. Remove fishing line from ponds and streams. Hooks, line, and lures are deadly to waterfowl.
9. Don't use pesticides on your lawn and avoid using chemicals outside your home.
10. Dispose of oil and antifreeze properly. If your car has a fluid leak, clean it up immediately.
11. Be alert when driving in rural areas and especially if you see a dead animal on the road. Many animals such as opossums, crows, and hawks will scavenge for food and may become roadkill themselves.
12. Place caps on chimneys and screens on dryer vents to keep out birds and raccoons.
13. Check trees for nests or dens before cutting or trimming. Leave hollow trunks standing as natural nesting sites.
14. Don't use glue traps and fly paper outdoors, in barns, or in attics. You may catch birds and bats.
15. Before starting vehicles that have been parked for a while, check for animals nesting in the engine compartment.
16. Wash all bird feeders once a week with a solution of one part bleach to thirty parts water. This helps prevent the spread of diseases such as conjunctivitis, which is a very contagious eye infection.
17. Move turtles off the road but DO NOT relocate them. Box turtles thrive <u>ONLY</u> in their immediate, original habitat.

18. Leave baby animals alone. If you think an animal is in distress, call your local wildlife rehabilitator BEFORE interfering. What you are witnessing may be normal behavior.
19. Provide habitat for wildlife by planting gardens and naturalizing your property. (See 2 above.)
20. Support your local wildlife rehabilitator!

IMPRINTING, TAMING, AND HABITUATION

Most mammals and birds recognize their own species through a process called "imprinting." When an animal is very young, and its eyes begin to focus, it sees who is nurturing, feeding, and protecting it. By observing this individual, it gets a mental picture of who it is. This picture, or imprint, stays with the animal its entire life, and once formed, it cannot be changed.

Exactly when this happens depends on the species. Ducks and geese, for example, imprint almost immediately; and this is reinforced during the first weeks of life. A great horned owl's eyes begin to focus at about two weeks of age. Imprinting takes place shortly thereafter. Mammals' eyes open and focus at various stages in their development.

This imprint not only gives an animal its identity, it also serves to help it choose a mate later in life. This is why a blue bird doesn't attempt to mate with a blue jay, or a red fox with a gray fox. The wrong species doesn't match the animal's imprint. An animal is looking for a mate that looks "JUST LIKE MOM."

Most of the time this works quite well: geese raise geese, crows raise crows, and deer raise deer. However, when a person hand-raises a wild animal, that animal can grow up believing it is a person. It will seek out people when it wants company, when it is injured or scared, and when it's time to mate.

It is a very miserable life for an animal that is imprinted on humans. It faces a life of frustration and rejection. Just think what it would be like if you were physically incompatible with everyone to whom you were attracted.

Even if the animal is past the age of imprinting and learns to accept humans, without others of its species with which to interact, it never learns the proper etiquette of behaving around other animals. An animal that doesn't use the proper body language and behavior will be rejected by other members of its own species.

Wildlife rehabilitators deal with the problems of imprinting in numerous ways, some of which are discussed below.

Surrogates

Wildlife rehabilitators often have a selection of non-releasable adult animals that can serve as foster parents for orphaned babies. The babies grow up with a natural parent and learn proper behavior and the skills they will need to survive.

Strength in numbers

Because wildlife rehabilitators receive large numbers of animals from the surrounding area, baby animals don't have to grow up alone. They are placed with other babies of their species that are in the same situation. Together they grow and bond and learn to interact. Once old enough to be released, they are released together as a family unit.

A network of rehabilitators

Wildlife rehabilitators network with one another. If a rehabilitator receives a single baby, it can be placed with another rehabilitator who has others of that species.

CATS VS. WILDLIFE

How many cats are there in the United States?

The estimated number of pet cats in urban and rural regions of the United States has grown from 30 million in 1970 to 86 million in 2016. These estimates include only those cats which people claim to "own" as pets, not cats that are semi-wild or free-ranging. Nationwide, approximately 35% of households have cats. In rural areas where free-ranging cats are usually not regarded as pets, approximately 60% of households have cats. The combined total of pet and free-ranging cats in the U.S. is probably more than 50 million.

What effects do domestic cats have on wildlife?

Although rural cats take the greatest toll, even urban house pets take live prey when allowed outside. Small mammals make up approximately 70% of these cats' prey while birds make up about 20%. The remaining 10% is a variety of other animals.

Observation of free-ranging domestic cats shows that some individuals can kill over one thousand wild animals per year. Nationwide, rural cats probably kill over one billion small mammals and hundreds of millions of birds each year. Urban and suburban cats add to this toll. Some of these kills are house mice, rats, and other species that are considered pests, but many are native songbirds and mammals whose populations are already stressed by other factors, such as habitat destruction and pesticide pollution.

Worldwide, cats may have been involved in the extinction of more bird species than any other factor except habitat destruction. Cats are contributing to the endangerment of populations of birds such as least terns, piping plovers, and loggerhead shrikes. In Florida, marsh rabbits in Key West have been threatened by predation from domestic cats. Cats introduced by people living on the barrier islands of Florida's coast have depleted several unique species of mice and woodrats to near extinction.

The effect on native predators

Not only do cats prey on many small mammals and birds, they can also outnumber and compete with native predators. Domestic cats eat many of the same animals as native predators. When present in large numbers, cats can reduce the availability of prey for native predators, such as hawks. Free-ranging domestic cats may also transmit new diseases to wild animals. Domestic cats have spread feline leukemia virus to mountain lions and may have recently infected the endangered Florida panther with feline panleukopenia (commonly known as feline distemper, an immune deficiency disease). These diseases may pose a serious threat to these rare species. Some free-ranging domestic cats also carry several diseases that are easily transmitted to humans, including rabies and toxoplasmosis.

Because many cats are protected and fed by humans, their population is not checked by natural occurrences such as disease, predation, and scarcity of wild game.

The effect on cats

The average life span of an indoor house cat is about fifteen years. A free-roaming domestic cat can be expected to live only between one and two years. This is due to disease, injuries, infection resulting from fights with wild animals and other cats, gunshots, and automobile accidents. Domestic cats are also one of the favored foods of the eastern coyote and the great horned owl. Keeping a cat indoors not only protects local wildlife, but also the cat and the people with whom the cat comes into contact.

The effect on people

Rabies is a virus that attacks the central nervous system of warm-blooded animals, including humans. Once it reaches the final symptomatic stage, it is 100% fatal. Cats are one of the most common carriers of rabies, and many rural cats are not vaccinated. Because of their close association with people and other domestic animals, cats pose a greater risk of transmitting rabies to humans and other pets than do wild rabies vector species such as raccoons, skunks, foxes, woodchucks, coyotes, and bats.

How you can help

People who have pet cats

- Keep only as many pets as you can control and care for.
- Keep domestic cats indoors.
- Spay and neuter all cats.
- Vaccinate all cats regularly.
- Place bird feeders away from areas where cats can hide and stalk birds.
- Leash-train your cat for outdoor exercise.

Farmers who need barnyard cats for rodent control

- Keep only as many cats as are needed to control rodent populations.

- Spay and neuter all cats. Spayed female cats are more likely to stay close to farm buildings.
- Vaccinate all cats regularly.
- Place owl boxes near barns to attract natural predators.

FEEDING WILDLIFE

Do you enjoy watching wildlife "up close and personal?" Most people who feed wildlife do so because they love animals and enjoy the interaction. Feeding wildlife becomes a regular hobby, and the hobbyist believes that the animals benefit from the experience.

Feeding wildlife is actually destructive and dangerous for the wild animals that are being fed. People who feed wildlife do not realize the danger into which they are placing the animals. The loving act of feeding wildlife becomes a selfish love where the only one who truly benefits is the person doing the feeding.

Overpopulation

The number of young a pair of animals produces is in direct proportion to the amount of food available. When food is unnaturally added to an area, the animals will overpopulate that area very quickly. Once the area is overpopulated, animals will compete for a limited number of nesting areas. When natural nesting areas aren't available, the animals invade houses and other buildings, becoming a nuisance.

Habitat contamination

When large numbers of animals habituate an area, that area can become contaminated quickly with feces, which fosters disease and bacteria. Nature, however, balances itself very well. A particular habitat has only enough food for a certain number of animals. Once that food supply is gone, the animals will move to a new habitat BEFORE the ground becomes saturated to the point of becoming unhealthy. Once the animals have left, the earth cleans itself through enzymes and microbial activity, and a new food supply grows. The rejuvenated habitat can once again support wildlife, and the animals return to start the cycle over.

A classic example of this pertains to ducks and geese. Botulism, a paralytic bacteria-produced illness, often develops on the bottom of ponds and lakes when the number of birds in the area is unnaturally high due to supplemental feeding. A heavy rain on a hot summer day will bring the contaminants to the surface, and entire flocks of birds can be affected and die.

Spread of disease

Diseases in wildlife are kept in check because animals usually do not associate with each other closely in the wild. Diseases will spread rapidly through animals who gather near a food supply. Rabies and distemper can spread among mammals simply by their eating from the same dishes. Mammals are not the only animals affected. Avian conjunctivitis is an extremely contagious eye infection that affects songbirds, especially sparrows. This disease is easily spread by birds gathering and sharing food at bird feeders.

Nutrition

Animals who routinely eat an unnatural diet often suffer from dietary problems. Foods commonly fed to them by people are often nutritionally inadequate. In infants and juveniles, growth and developmental problems result in crippling deformities that are often fatal. Adults can suffer from digestive problems, serious health conditions, and behavioral disturbances.

Safety

Another reason to avoid feeding wild animals is to ensure that they retain their fear of humans. YOU may not pose a threat to their survival, but if they do not fear ALL humans, they are bound to encounter an unfriendly one sooner or later.

So, What Can You Do?

You can enjoy wildlife visiting your backyard with some positive changes. Instead of supplying food, supply **habitat**: an increasingly limited commodity.

In today's ever-changing world, habitat loss is the number-one reason for distressed wildlife. Planned landscaping that includes the addition of natural food-bearing plants as well as nesting and hiding places, will attract wildlife without disrupting its natural routines.

For example, hummingbird feeders supply energy with no nutrition. Leaving a hummingbird feeder out too late in the season can "trap" them in an area after migration. Planting nectar-producing flowers will attract hummingbirds to your garden, supplying them with nutritionally-rich foods that will disappear when it's time for the birds to migrate.

WILD PETS

People who find animals can be very tempted to raise them or keep them as pets. There is a multitude of reasons why this is a BAD decision.

We've already covered the many risks to you, your family, and pets through contact with wildlife. Keeping wildlife in your home for any period of time increases these risks each day that you share your home with a wild animal.

I've also touched on the emotional damage animals suffer through imprinting (see page 102).

In addition, wild animals need special, experienced care. They require specific nutrition, medical attention, and housing.

MILK FORMULAS FOR BABY ANIMALS.

We are often presented with baby animals after people have fed milk to them for days or weeks before bringing them to us. Often these babies are suffering digestive distress and malnutrition. Before you decide to feed milk to that baby animal, please consider the complexity involved.

Each species of animal has different nutritional requirements for proper development including the fat/protein ratio of its milk. Milk designed for cats (carnivores, or meat-eaters) is high in protein so the kitten can develop strong bones and muscles more slowly. Bunnies (herbivores, or plant-eaters) need high-fat content to grow very quickly and do not need the high protein of a carnivore diet. Thus, feeding kitten milk to bunnies (which suggestion we often see on various websites) is incorrect.

These squirrels are the same age, but the one in the center was fed Similac, a human baby formula, for five days by the person who found it. That baby eventually died.

In addition to having the right milk formulation, the correct amount needs to be fed at proper intervals. Most baby animals' stomach capacity is a percentage of their body weight; and this varies by species. Babies must be weighed daily to determine the proper serving amounts. If the wrong amount is given, the animal will become a victim of either diarrhea (from too much) or starvation (from too little). Caloric intake must also be monitored to make sure the animal has the energy to grow properly. The caloric-intake calculation for a baby mammal is 70 x W.75 x S = Kcals/24 hours (W = weight in kilograms) (S = stress factor). The stress factor is determined by the age and health of the animal.

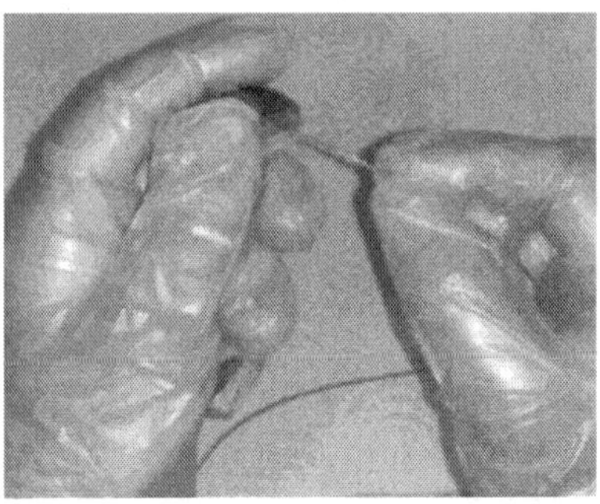

Other considerations in successfully raising a baby animal include feeding methods, conspecific digestive enzymes, habitat enrichment, stimulation for elimination, and imprinting.

As you can see, raising baby wildlife is a science, and the animals, who are living, feeling creatures, deserve more than trial and error or guesses.

When you are tempted to take a wild animal home to be a pet, ask yourself these questions:

- Is what I'm doing legal?
- Am I willing to risk the health, and possibly the lives, of myself, my family, and my pets?
- Am I properly trained in the care of this species of animal?
- Can I obtain veterinary care for this animal? (*Veterinarians will not treat wildlife that is possessed unlawfully*)
- Am I willing to risk killing the animal because I may not truly know how to care for it?
- Am I willing to change my lifestyle to accommodate the animal's natural and unalterable behavior?

If you cannot truthfully answer "yes" to <u>EACH</u> question, please do not attempt to keep a wild animal as a pet.

NUISANCE WILDLIFE

There are times when the animal that is found is not in danger but is in itself, the problem.

As civilization spreads, we are encroaching more and more upon wild animal habitat. Animals either adapt or perish, and in today's world, many are adapting. An urban area is a wildlife mecca, and species thought to be strictly rural, such as the red fox, are becoming urbanized. As the human population increases, this cohabitation will become even more pronounced.

Animals are extremely opportunistic and will inhabit homes and backyards because shelter and food are plentiful and life is easy. It may be enjoyable to watch a pair of squirrels playing and jumping acrobatically through the trees in your backyard. It is quite another thing when you've discovered that they are living in the walls of your home.

When faced with a nuisance wild animal in or near your home, first make sure that you are not causing the problem. Are you doing anything to attract the animal? Are you feeding one type of animal and have, unknowingly, opened a buffet for all?

Bird feeders are often the cause of many uninvited wild animal guests. The food not only attracts squirrels that can climb the feeders, but it also falls to the ground attracting ducks, geese, raccoons, bears, and rodents such as rats and mice.

Cat food put out for the neighborhood felines is a request for all the area skunks, raccoons, and opossums to come calling.

Before taking desperate measures to rid your property of nuisance animals, scrutinize your own behavior and that of your close neighbors to be sure you are not creating the problem. If you are, please discontinue the practice!

BIRD FEEDER BANDITS

We often get complaints about two problem animals in regards to bird feeders: squirrels and hawks. Let's talk about hawks first.

When you put out bird food, you are attracting a large number and variety of songbirds to a small area. For the animals that prey upon songbirds, that means you've gathered together a vast variety of food for them, and the chances of a successful hunt at this location are good.

There is only one way to stop a hawk from being a constant watchman over your yard – stop feeding the birds. You have to stop feeding for several weeks until the hawk moves on to other hunting grounds. If the hawk lives and nests locally, you will need to stop feeding indefinitely.

Another way to deal with the situation is to look at it differently. If you put food out to attract wildlife activity to your yard, then you have been extremely successful. When you feed the birds, you feed ALL the birds, including the hawks. Enjoy the opportunity to witness wildlife at its greatest. Life in the wild can be brutal, but that is the essence of nature.

Squirrels are frequent thieves of the bird feeder, emptying the contents quickly and even destroying feeders to get at the food. "Squirrel-proof" bird feeders do not always work and can be expensive.

One trick that often helps keep squirrels away is to lace the bird seed liberally with powdered red pepper. The taste is a deterrent for rodents, and the birds don't seem to even notice.

BIRDS ATTACKING WINDOWS

A common songbird problem during nesting season is birds attacking windows. The culprit is usually a male bird, and frequently a cardinal.

The cause is quite simple; this confused bird sees his reflection in the window and thinks it's a competitor male out to take over his nesting area. He becomes obsessed with chasing it away and consequently flies at his own reflection.

If this were a real bird and not his own reflection, such behavior would quickly end with the weaker bird leaving the area. With his reflection, however, he is met with equal action, and it is a stalemate. His obsession can become so great that he never attracts a mate, never nests, and may injure or kill himself colliding with the window.

The cure to this problem is also quite simple; you must remove his reflection. The easiest way is to allow the windows to remain "dirty" because only clean windows reflect well. Reflection from a clean window can be eliminated by spraying with soapy or salty water and allowing it to dry. A more permanent solution is to install dark screening on the outside of the windows.

We've even heard stories of this behavior toward cars. Birds have been reported attacking side-view mirrors, windows, and shiny paint. The same concept applies. Although you would not want to spray salty water on your car, can the car be garaged or draped when parked? A cloth draped over a mirror will eliminate the attractiveness of the mirror.

BIRDS THAT FLY AT YOU

Another common problem during nesting season is birds dive-bombing people as they enter and exit a doorway. Typically, this is a bird nesting nearby that feels threatened by your presence. This activity usually occurs when there are eggs or hatchlings in the nest.

Try to determine what species of bird it is and the location of the nest. The species will give you an indication as to where the nest is located and how long the nesting period lasts. Depending on the species, incubation is generally one to three weeks.

When the eggs hatch and the parents are busy gathering food for their hungry offspring, this activity may or may not cease.

If you can enter and exit by way of another door, that would be the simplest solution. If this is not possible, setting a visual barrier between the doorway and the nest, such as a dressing blind or a sheet, may give the birds a feeling of security.

WOODPECKERS ATTACKING WOODEN HOMES

Woodpeckers peck wood – that's what they do, and it's why they are so named. The echo of rhythmic drumming on a country morning is a wonderful sound – unless the wood being drilled is part of your home! Woodpecker damage can be quite extensive and expensive, but it can be prevented.

When a woodpecker drums, it is actually looking for insects hiding under tree bark. If you have an insect infestation of the wood, these birds will come calling and can alert you to the problem. An inspection by an exterminator may be in order.

If there are no insects, but a bird is determined to dismantle your home, bright yellow balloons hung on the side of the home usually will chase it away. Mylar balloons will hold up better in the weather, but you want to utilize the bright yellow color. Attach the balloon to the side or corner of your home with a one-to-two-foot line which will allow the balloon to move with the breeze. You may need to hang one on each outside wall to protect the entire building.

SQUIRRELS IN YOUR HOME

Squirrels living inside the walls of a house present a very dangerous situation. These destructive rodents can chew on wiring and have caused electrical house fires.

High-frequency sound emitters, mothballs, pepper sprays, and animal deterrents only work for a short time, if at all. Removing the housing and food source is the best way to prevent squirrel damage to your home.

Move bird feeders at least twenty feet from the house, promptly remove all outdoor pet foods, keep your barbecue clean (including the drip pan), and keep garbage in tightly closed metal cans.

Examine your home for entrance areas and seal the area with half-inch hardware cloth. Once squirrels get inside your home, the only real solution is to relocate them. Do not trap during the squirrels' nesting season so you do not separate a mother squirrel from her babies, or you will have a second wildlife emergency on your hands. Gray squirrels typically have two litters per year, one in the early spring and one in the late summer to fall. Early summer is often the best time to relocate squirrels.

Squirrels can be live-trapped out of the area either by you or by a wildlife pest control person. Before attempting to trap squirrels yourself, contact the state wildlife agency where you live to be certain you can legally trap the animals.

Traps can be purchased or rented from local hardware stores. Live traps for squirrels are about 5 x 5 x 18 inches long with one door and ½ x 1-inch wire spacing. Sizing is important; a live trap with the wrong dimensions will not catch any squirrels. Wire spacing that is too large a size can injure a squirrel.

Extra-crunchy peanut butter is excellent bait for squirrels, as are a variety of shelled nuts. Bait and place the trap in the area where the squirrels generally run and check the trap several times each day, especially in the morning and the evening.

Once the squirrel is captured, drive it to a wilderness habitat with a large variety of nut-bearing trees (such as oak) at least five miles from your home. Be careful releasing squirrels, as they have long, sharp, curved teeth that can cause a serious puncture.

RACCOONS IN THE CHIMNEY OR ATTIC

Raccoons can live in chimneys and attics for long periods without detection. The first sign is often the sound of babies that are a few weeks old.

Raccoons can be encouraged to leave a denning area, such as a shed or attic, by making their stay uncomfortable. They prefer a dark, quiet location, so turn on the lights and turn up the music. By placing a loud radio in the attic and turning on bright lights, you will compel the mother to find a new location. It may take her a few days, but soon she will move all the babies and vacate. Once she has left with the babies, seal off all entrance points to prevent further problems.

Raccoons in chimneys are a bit more difficult and require the installation of a chimney cap. Make sure there are no animals inside the chimney, or they will be trapped and starve or may even enter your home. Raccoons need to be live-trapped and relocated before you install a chimney cap.

Raccoons can also be relocated by a professional urban wildlife pest control expert. Ask the company about the method of disposal. Some states require professionally trapped animals to be destroyed.

RABBITS IN THE GARDEN

Rabbits can easily be kept from eating gardens and the bark from trees by removing cover where they hide and installing

fencing. Fencing to exclude rabbits needs to be at least two feet high and have a maximum of one-inch-square wire spacing.

Also, use the wildlife repellent recipe on the next page 117.

SKUNK ODOR NEUTRALIZER

One quart of 3% hydrogen peroxide
¼ cup of baking soda
One teaspoon of liquid soap

Mix ingredients only when ready to use the neutralizer and apply immediately to affected area. Massage into the area for about two minutes. Rinse with water.

DO NOT STORE THE SOLUTION! If you put it into a capped container, it may explode!

WILDLIFE REPELLENT RECIPE

from Carol Martino

This recipe works well on mammals. The solution must be applied every two weeks and after it rains until the problem is resolved.

Ingredients:

- 1 whole Spanish onion
- 1 jalapeno pepper
- 1 tablespoon cayenne pepper
- 2 quarts of water

Directions:
Chop up the onion and the jalapeno pepper.
Add the cayenne pepper.
Mix these together and boil in 2 quarts of water for about 20 minutes.
Let cool, then strain the water through cheesecloth.
Using a garden sprayer, spray any area outside where wild animals or even neighborhood pets are being a nuisance.
This process may have to be carried out for a period of two weeks to ensure success.
This mixture is non-toxic and will not harm any animal, but it will succeed in keeping them away.

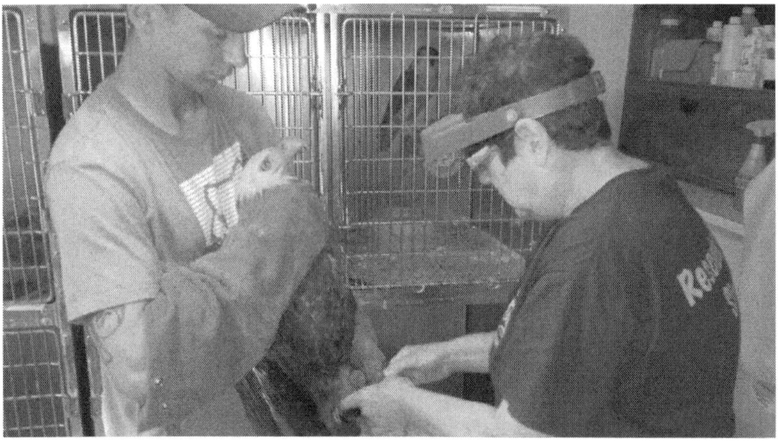

ABOUT WILDLIFE REHABILITATION

Wildlife rehabilitation consists of a network of individuals and organizations that care for injured, sick, and orphaned wild animals with the goal of releasing these animals back into their natural habitats. Wildlife rehabilitators have demonstrated a proficient knowledge of wildlife by passing both written and oral examinations, have met certain housing standards for species they are permitted to treat, attend continuing education classes, and work with a licensed veterinarian.

Through rehabilitation, an animal is given the benefits of proper nutrition and husbandry as well as modern medical care which includes fluid and drug therapy, diagnostics, x-rays, and surgery. For animals that cannot survive in the wild, or that are beyond the ability to recover, rehabilitation offers a painless end to their suffering.

Individuals who unlawfully possess wildlife not only endanger the health and well-being of that animal but also risk their own health, as well as the health of their family and pets. In addition to the physical injury a wild animal can inflict, wildlife carries diseases and parasites that can infect humans and domestic animals. Furthermore, animals that have been humanized pose a great threat to the people they encounter as well as to themselves.

By offering an alternative, wildlife rehabilitation is also a public service which provides the public with a humane, legal way of dealing with the wildlife in need that they encounter. The person who finds and rescues a wild animal is the first step in the process of returning an animal to its natural habitat, as well as in protecting the public health. From the moment you pick up an animal in distress, you become part of that network of individuals whose purpose is to give that animal a second chance at life.

WHY ARE THERE SO FEW REHABILITATORS?

Although we are a country that purports to love and protect our wildlife, there is NO state or federal funding for wildlife rehabilitation. Governmental agencies heavily regulate the activity, but they do not support it.

Most wildlife rehabilitators not only don't get paid for their services, but they must also raise the funding to support their work. Many have outside employment to cover the cost of rehabilitation in addition to their own living expenses. It is difficult for any person to devote the time, space, and money to rehabilitate wildlife properly.

Those who dedicate their lives to the hundreds, even thousands, of animals that come through their doors each year do so because of a deep devotion to their charges.

FIND A LOCAL WILDLIFE REHABILITATOR

If you've been directed to this page, then you have a true wildlife emergency or need further advice from a wildlife rehabilitator.

I have attempted to supply as much information as possible to get you started, and all the internet resources and contact numbers listed are current as of this book's publication date.

The entities I've listed on the following pages have been around for a long time and are extremely helpful. You can also find other resources by doing an internet search for "find a wildlife rehabilitator."

Wildlife rehabilitators do not generally advertise their services, and it is rare to find one listed in the Yellow Pages. Funds are usually limited, and the expense of advertising is a luxury most rehabilitators cannot afford.

Rehabilitators do, however, network with local veterinarians and animal shelters. The local 911 center may also have a number on file for wildlife emergencies.

Licensed wildlife rehabilitators are regulated by two governing bodies: the state fish and game or conservation department; and, if they work with migratory birds, the US Fish and Wildlife Service. These organizations can be found in the "Blue Pages" of your telephone directory. They can also be found by doing an internet search for your state, plus wildlife protection.

Keep in mind that you may have to make several phone calls before finding a rehabilitator close to you who may be able to help. Please be patient and persistent – that animal is relying on YOU!

INTERNET RESOURCES

RED CREEK LINKS

www.RedCreekWildlifeCenter.com

The official site for Red Creek provides links and search features for locating wildlife rehabilitators.

www.WildlifeEDU.com

A division of Red Creek Wildlife Center, Wildlife EDU offers online classes for those interested in volunteering or becoming licensed to rehabilitate wildlife.

www.PAWR.org

The Pennsylvania Association of Wildlife Rehabilitators has a current list of all licensed wildlife rehabilitators in the state.

www.RescuingWildlife.com

Based on this book, the key found at the beginning of this book is also available on the web.

OTHER LINKS

www.ahnow.org

Animal Help Now is a 24-hour search engine, available as a website and as a free phone app, to assist with the full range of animal-related emergencies, including finding a local wildlife rehabilitator.

www.nwrawildlife.org

The National Wildlife Rehabilitators Association publishes up-to-date documents on its website of the current state and federal agencies regulating wildlife rehabilitation.

www.theiwrc.org

The International Wildlife Rehabilitation Council. It contains some suggestions for common wildlife issues and has a search area for rehabilitators.

www.humanesociety.org

The Humane Society of the United States publishes a current list of state organizations along with links to wildlife rehabilitators organized by state.

ABOUT THE AUTHOR

A wildlife rehabilitator since 1991, Peggy Hentz is the founder of Red Creek Wildlife Center, Inc and a member of the Pennsylvania Rehabilitation and Education Advisory Council.

She has developed the wildlife rehabilitation certification programs for threatened and endangered species in Pennsylvania and wildlife capture and transport in Pennsylvania and New Jersey.

Peggy is the author of "Rescuing Wildlife, A Guide to Injured and Orphaned Animals," published by Stackpole Books (version one of this book) and two children's books, "Zoey Finds a Bunny Nest" and "Zoey Finds a Fawn."

Peggy's most recent project is www.WildlifeEDU.com which offers online training opportunities for wildlife rehabilitators and volunteers.

Printed in Great Britain
by Amazon

58432134R00079